A

RUSSIA

'In Brief': Books for Busy People

by Anne Davison

Copyright2018 Anne Davison

Cover Design by Karen Turner

OTHER BOOKS BY THE SAME AUTHOR

A History of Central Asia

A History of China

Abraham's Children: Jew, Christian, Muslim; Commonality and
Conflict

From the Medes to the Mullahs: a History of Iran

Making Sense of Militant Islam

Paul of Tarsus: a First Century Radical

The Holy Roman Empire: Power Politics Papacy

The Mughal Empire

The Ottoman Empire

*****

http://www.inbriefbooks.com

CONTENTS

MAPS

*****

PREFACE

October 2017 marked one hundred years since the Russian Revolution and the overthrow of the Romanov Dynasty. But as the anniversary approached, there appeared to be some ambivalence in the Kremlin as to how the event should be celebrated, if indeed, celebrated at all.

The mood in Russia was captured in Shaun Walker's enlightening article entitled *Tragedy or triumph? Russians agonise over how to mark 1917 revolutions'.* Published in *The Guardian* newspaper on the 17th December 2016, the article reveals the dilemma facing President Putin and those charged with arranging anniversary events.

The article reports the words of journalist Michael Zygar, who said: *"There is no officially approved narrative of 1917; it's too difficult and complicated. But it's a very important period to help understand what's happening in Russia now, and very important for the national consciousness"*

Zygar continued: *"There's no official line from the Kremlin – they can't identify themselves with Lenin, because he was a revolutionary, and they can't identify with Nicholas II because he was a weak leader.'* This goes some way to explaining the problem facing President Putin. He would not want to celebrate the life of either a revolutionary or a weakling.

It could be said that the Soviet experiment was simply a blip in the long history of the Russian people and nationalities ruled from Moscow or Leningrad. But how, or why did the blip happen? More significantly, is the blip slowly being forgotten, while people and events from Russia's 'glorious' past are re-emerging into the Russian consciousness?

There are signs that this may be the case. Stalin has been brought in from the cold and a monument to Vladimir the Great has been erected outside the Kremlin. Even a monument of Ivan the Terrible has been unveiled on the grounds that through his expansionist policies he increased Russia's territory. And the

Russian Orthodox Church has been reinstated, not only as a moral force but also as a support of the Russian State.

This book is an attempt to look back at Russian history and to try and discover why these particular rulers are so relevant today. Perhaps it might then be possible to identify those characteristics, traits and trends that not only survived the Soviet period, but re-emerged as strong as ever.

As with other books in the 'In Brief' series, this book is aimed at the general reader who wants to understand a particular historical topic but does not have the time or inclination to read a heavy academic tome. With this mind, footnotes have been omitted.

While there will inevitably be gaps in a book of this size, the intention is to cover the most significant events that moulded Russian history. Should the reader be inspired to further reading on the subject, a small selection of the main works that have been consulted is provided at the end.

Where possible, maps and charts are provided which should help the reader navigate through the text. A 'Who's Who and What's What' is included at the end of the book.

Finally, I would like to thank those friends and colleagues who gave of their valuable time to read through various chapters, proof read the text, and offer helpful comments and advice.

*****

CHAPTER ONE

The Kievan Rus'

We get most of our information about the peoples who first populated the region of today's Russia from the *Russian Primary Chronicle,* also known as the *Chronicle of Nestor,* the *Kiev Chronicle* or *The Tale of Bygone Years.* Nestor, a monk from Kiev, is said to have compiled the chronicle in the year 1113, taking sources from Byzantine chronicles, Slav literature, official documents and popular oral sagas. While the original document has been lost, there are extant copies, the earliest being dated 1377. It is now generally thought that the Chronicle was not the work of one author, but more likely to have been the joint effort of several chroniclers.

The *Russian Primary Chronicle* covers the period from 850 to 1110 and tells the history of the Kievan Rus'. It includes the arrival of the Vikings, or Varangians from Scandinavia, their integration with the Eastern Slavs, the Christianisation of the Rus' under Vladimir the Great in 988 and the Rus' invasions of Constantinople.

Nestor also relates in his Chronicle how the apostle St Andrew preached in the area of the Black Sea and founded the See of Constantinople. According to the Chronicle, the Saint then travelled up the Dnieper River as far as Kiev where he planted a cross on the site of the current St Andrew's Church of Kiev. St Andrew is now patron saint of both Russia and Ukraine.

The Slavs

The history of Russia began in the 9th Century in the Baltic region, an area incorporating today's Latvia, Lithuania, Belarus and Ukraine, populated then by Finnic and Slavic tribes. Today the Slavs are the largest Indo-European ethno-linguistic group in Europe. Speaking a variety of Slavic languages, they are the native population of most of Central and Eastern Europe, North Asia and Central Asia.

The Slavs are usually categorised into West Slavs (Czechs, Poles and Slovaks), East Slavs (Belarusians, Russians and Ukrainians) and South Slavs (people of the Balkans including Slovenes and Bulgarians). There is also a theory that the English word 'slave' is derived from the word Slav in reference to the Slavs from the Balkans who were taken as slaves by Muslims, particularly during the Ottoman period. In relation to Russian history and the subject of this book, the East Slavs are of most interest to us.

There is very little written information about the Slavs before the 11th Century. However, it is generally thought that the various Slavic tribes probably migrated westwards, from Central Asia into Eastern Europe, in the wake of the great migrations of the Huns, Avars, Alans and Magyars, which occurred between the 6th and 10th Centuries. They then settled in forests and on the banks of the Rivers Danube and Dnieper as well as around the Black Sea.

The first mention of the Slavs appeared in Byzantine chronicles during the reign of Byzantine Emperor Justinian I who reigned from 527 to 565. At that time, the historian and legal adviser named Procopius of Caesarea, mentions the Sclaveni and Antae tribes who were thought to be Slavs. Procopius was adviser to the renowned Byzantine General Belisarius and he accompanied the General on most of his campaigns. In his writings Procopius refers to Slavic tribes invading Constantinople. Further Slavic invasions of Constantinople are mentioned in Byzantine chronicles during the reign of Emperor Michael III who reigned between 842 and 867.

The Slav tribes lived in autonomous groups, each having a democratically elected leader. They survived by hunting, fishing and bee-keeping and as agriculturists they practiced a policy of slash and burn. Consequently, because the soil deteriorated, they were forced to move every few years.

Nestor's Chronicle describes the Slavs as having wooden bathhouses that they warmed to an extreme heat. They *'then undress, and after anointing themselves with an acid liquid, they take young branches and lash their bodies. They actually lash themselves so violently that they barely escape alive'.*

The Eastern Slavs, forerunners of today's Russians, Ukrainians and Belorusians were pagans. Their primary god was Perun, who was god of thunder and lightning. He was also associated with fire, mountains, wind and the oak, which in Slavic mythology was a sacred tree symbolising the world. Another popular symbol of the god was the 'axe of Perun'. The *Primary Chronicle* records how, in 907, the Slavic ruler Prince Oleg sealed a peace treaty with the Byzantines by swearing an oath in the name of Perun and his weapons.

The Slavic tribes were not warlike people and consequently found themselves forced to pay tribute to other, more powerful and aggressive tribes such as the Khazars and Pechenegs. In order to survive they were also forced to pay tribute to roving bands of Scandinavians, or Vikings.

The Vikings

The Vikings, who were from Denmark, Norway and Sweden, were sea faring people who have been known by various names. To the people of the British Isles they were known as the 'Danes', to the Francs they were referred to as 'Normans', meaning 'north men'. The people of Ireland called them 'Galls', meaning 'strangers' and to the people of Eastern Europe they were known as Rus', thought to mean 'rowers' in recognition of their expertise as seafarers.

It is generally thought that the Rus' who migrated to Eastern Europe originated from the coastal region of Sweden. One group of Rus' adventurers travelled as far as Constantinople where they formed an elite bodyguard to the Byzantine Emperor, known as the Varangian Guard.

For climatic reasons, as well as the problem of overpopulation, the young and more adventurous Vikings were frequently migrated. While the Danes and Normans conquered territory in Northern Europe, the Rus' moved into Eastern Europe primarily as traders. They travelled as far as Constantinople trading in furs, amber and slaves in exchange for silks and manufactured goods. By making use of the great lakes and rivers of northeast Europe they were able to travel the whole journey almost entirely by water. If they had to travel short distances on land between rivers or lakes, or around rapids, they carried their longboats across land, a practice called portage.

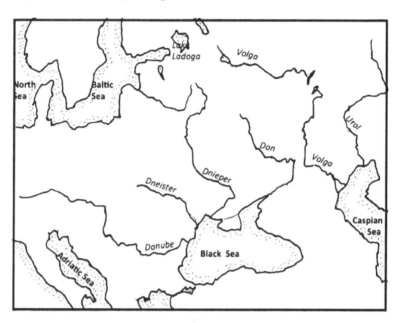

Rurik: 862-879

In around the year 862, the Slavic and Finnic tribes rebelled against the Rus' and drove them back across the Baltic Sea. However, when in-fighting broke out, they decided to ask the Rus' to return. According to the *Russian Primary Chronicle*, the Slav tribes appealed to the Rus' with the words "*Our land is vast and abundant, but there is no order in it. Come and reign as princes and have authority over us!*" Whether or not this is a true account is debatable, but the story has become part of Russian folk law.

The chronicles record that a Rus' chieftain named Rurik accepted the invitation. Together with two of his brothers and their extended families, Rurik settled in the region of Novgorod and reigned over the tribes. He governed the city of Novgorod while his brothers Sineus and Truvor ruled Belorussia and Izborsk respectively.

When Rurik's brothers died he acquired their lands and became Grand Prince. This marked the foundation of the Rurik Dynasty that was to last until 1612 with the death of Vasili IV of Russia. The Rurik Dynasty, which spanned some 700 years, was then succeeded by the House of Romanov, which ruled until 1917 with the abdication of Tsar Nicholas II.

According to the *Russian Primary Chronicle,* before Rurik died in 879, he nominated his male relative Oleg as his successor. Rurik also placed his young son Igor under the guardianship of Oleg until the boy came of age. Other sources, for example the *Novgorod First Chronicle,* written around 1110, as well as letters written at the time by members of the Khazar dynasty, give different accounts. They make no mention of the relationship between Rurik, Oleg and Igor and they record a different dating. Despite these differing sources and also disagreements among historians, that offered by the *Russian Primary Chronicle,* is the

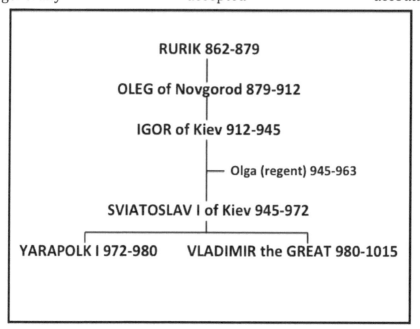

Oleg: 879-912

Oleg came to power at a time when the economy of the Novgorod region was weak. He therefore needed to gain access to the lucrative trade route from Scandinavia to Constantinople, known as 'from the Varangians to the Greeks'

Oleg gathered warriors from the surrounding Finnic and Slavic tribes and seized the towns of Smolensk and Lyubech. Having garrisoned both with his men, he then moved down the Dnieper River until he reached Kiev in around 882. At that time Askold and Dir, who were thought to be Rus' leaders previously under the command of Rurik, ruled the city. Oleg challenged their legitimacy and presented the young Igor as rightful heir to Rurik.

After murdering Askold and Dir, Oleg then decided that Kiev, being strategically well placed on the trade route, should be the new capital of the Rus'. He called the city 'the mother of Rus' towns' and proclaimed himself Grand Prince of Kiev. While the year 862 marks the beginning of the Rus' Dynasty under Rurik, the year 882 marks the foundation of Kievan Rus' by Oleg.

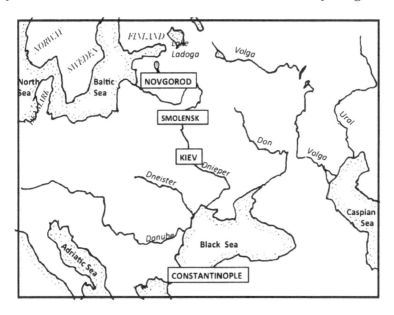

By 907, Oleg had consolidated his power and strengthened his military forces sufficiently to attempt an invasion of Constantinople. His armies laid siege to the city until the Byzantine Emperor agreed to a peace treaty, the terms of which included a regular tribute payable by the Byzantines to the Kievan Rus' in exchange for military help.

Igor: 912-945

Igor succeeded Oleg as Grand Prince of Kiev and was crowned in 914. According to the *Russian Primary Chronicle* he ruled until 945, but some historians have challenged this date largely because we have very little information about the thirty years of his rule. What is apparent, however, is that he had a reputation for greed and was never as an effective ruler as his predecessor.

Although there are Muslim accounts of a Rus' presence in the region of the Caspian Sea during Igor's reign, both as traders and as raiders, there is no evidence that Igor was among them.

It is recorded, however, that Igor laid siege to Constantinople in 913. Byzantine sources also refer to a war with the Rus' that was led by Igor in 941. On that occasion, the Byzantines claim to have repelled the invaders with 'Greek fire', which was an incendiary weapon made of a napalm substance that could burn on water and therefore easily destroy ships.

During this same period, we are told that relations between the Byzantines and the Khazars were poor. The *Khazar Correspondence*, a series of letters exchanged between the Caliph of Cordoba and Joseph Khagan of the Khazars, tells how the Byzantine Emperor Romanus I Lecapenus had been persecuting the Jewish population of Khazaria. It has been suggested that the Khazars consequently sought the help of the Kievan Rus'. Igor and his allies responded to the request and invaded Byzantine territory when the Emperor's forces were fighting off the Muslims in the South and East of his Empire.

Igor's gruesome death in 945 is described by the Byzantine chronicler Leo the Deacon. According to Leo, he died at the hands of Drevlians, a warlike tribe of Eastern Slavs. Leo tells how he was captured while collecting tribute, *"They had bent down two birch trees to the prince's feet and tied them to his legs; then they let the trees straighten again, thus tearing the prince's body apart"*.

Igor's wife Olga meted out her revenge on the Drevlians and then assumed the Regency of the Kievan Rus' until her young son Sviatoslav came of age. Olga was to leave a far greater legacy in Russian history than that of her husband Igor.

Olga: regent 945-960

In an attempt to appease Olga for the murder of her husband, the Drevlians sent messengers with gifts and an offer of marriage to their Prince. But she was determined to hold on to power until her son was able to rule in his own right and she was also determined to avenge her husband's death. Her immediate response was to have the Drevlian messengers buried alive. On another occasion, she had messengers burned alive in a bathhouse.

It is also recorded that Olga demanded three sparrows and three pigeons from every house in the Drevlian capital city. She then had a flax tow tied to the tails of the birds. The tow was then lit and the birds released to fly back to their homes. In the chaos that ensued the inhabitants were burned alive in their homes. The survivors were taken as slaves.

Nestor then tells how some ten years later Olga went through a complete transformation. In 955 she travelled to Constantinople with the sole purpose of learning about the Christian Faith. She was baptised by the Greek Patriarch and took the Christian name Yelena, or Helena. The Byzantine Emperor acted as her godfather.

Helena was tireless in her efforts to spread Christianity among the Rus' but the full conversion of the people had to wait until the reign of her grandson Grand Prince Vladimir. To her great disappointment, her son Sviatoslav remained a pagan, claiming that his men would mock him if he adopted the religion of the Greeks.

Olga has come down in history as the first Apostle of the Russian people. The Eastern Orthodox Church, Roman Catholic Church, Eastern Catholic Church and the Ukrainian Greek Catholic Church all venerate her as a Saint. Her Feast Day is celebrated on the 11th July, which is the anniversary of her death in 969, at the age of 79 years.

Sviatoslav - ruled 945-972

Sviatoslav was the first Prince of the Rus' with a Slav, rather than a Norse, or Viking name, which is an indication that the two peoples were gradually integrating.

We get a glimpse of the man Sviatoslav from both the *Russian Primary Chronicle* and also the Byzantine historian Leo the Deacon. *The Primary Chronicle* tells how Sviatoslav had little time for administration and much preferred to be on campaign with his men, known as *druzhina*, roughly meaning 'Company'. He had no need of wagons, kettles or tents, preferring to sleep on a horse blanket using his saddle as a pillow. He and his men ate roasted horsemeat, game and beef.

Leo describes him as of average height but sturdy. He had blue eyes and a bushy moustache. He shaved his blond hair with the exception of a side-lock that was a sign of nobility. He was usually dressed in white and wore a single large earring that was decorated with a large gem and two pearls. This description was probably typical of most of the Rus' Princes of the time.

Sviatoslav's first campaign was in the East against the Khazar Empire. He persuaded the vassal tribes of the Khazars to change sides and join his army. He destroyed Khazar cities, including their capital Atil. With the destruction of the Khazars, Sviatoslav now had access to the lucrative north-south trade route across the Black Sea. At around the same time he succeeded in subjugating the warlike Pechenegs.

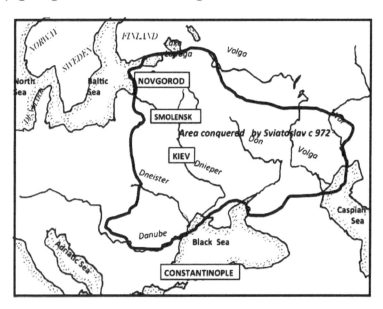

In around 967, the Byzantines were being threatened by the rise of the Bulgarian Empire on its borders. Consequently, Emperor Nikephoros offered the Rus' a large amount of gold in return for military help. With an army of around 60,000 men, including Pecheneg mercenaries, Sviatoslav succeeded in defeating the Bulgar ruler Boris.

To the consternation of Nikephoros, Sviatoslav showed no sign of returning to Kiev and started to settle in parts of Bulgaria. He moved the capital of the Rus' from Kiev to Pereyaslavets, a town on the mouth of the River Danube in present day Rumania. He announced that his new capital would be the centre of his lands, where "*all the riches would flow: gold, silks, wine, and various fruits from Greece, silver and horses from Hungary and Bohemia, and from Rus' furs, wax, honey, and slaves*".

Not surprisingly, this displeased the Byzantines. They attacked Kiev and persuaded the Pechenegs to assassinate Sviatoslav. Since the Pechenegs had previously suffered at the hands of the Grand Prince of the Rus', they gladly accepted the challenge. Sviatoslav was ambushed, killed and his skull made into a chalice by the Pecheneg khan.

Vladimir the Great - ruled 980-1015

Before Sviatoslav died in 972, he divided his kingdom between his three sons. His eldest son Yaropolk was made Prince of Kiev, which was the most important city. The second son, Oleg, became Prince of the Drevlians. Vladimir, who was the third son and the child of his father's mistress, was given Novgorod.

As so often happens in these situations, conflict broke out between the sons. Yaropolk murdered his younger brother and seized his territory. He then invaded Novgorod forcing Vladimir to flee to Scandinavia. With help from the ruler of Norway Vladimir managed to assemble a Varangian army of mercenaries and retake Novgorod. He then arranged the murder of Yarolpolk, retrieved the city of Kiev and forcibly married Yarolpolk's Greek widow.

By 980, Vladimir had united the principalities of the Kievan Rus' under his sole rule. He suppressed all rebellions, led campaigns against the Pechenegs and Volga Bulgars and built fortifications along the borders of a realm that stretched from the Baltic to the Black Sea.

Throughout this time, Vladimir remained a staunch pagan. He had numerous wives and concubines, built temples and statues to the pagan gods and it is said that he took part in rituals involving human sacrifice. But he is best known for the conversion of the people of Kievan Rus' to Christianity and it is for this act that he earned the title 'Vladimir the Great'.

There are different versions as to how this conversion came about. Several Christian and Muslim accounts claim that the Byzantine Emperor Basil II appealed to Vladimir for military help to put down a revolt. Vladimir agreed on condition that he was offered the Emperor's sister, Anna, in marriage. Basil agreed to the marriage but on condition that Vladimir and all the Rus' people first convert to Christianity. When the wedding arrangements were settled, Vladimir sent 6,000 troops to help put down the rebellion and he then arranged the baptism of the people of Kiev, Novgorod as well as the Pecheneg princes.

A more popular and colourful account of the conversion of the Rus' is given in the *Russian Primary Chronicle*. Here Nestor tells how, in the year 978, Vladimir sent his envoys to study the religion of other nations. The envoys reported that the Muslim Bulgarians *'had no gladness in them'* and that their religion would not suit the Rus' because alcohol and pork was forbidden, to which Vladimir responded *'Drinking is the joy of all Rus'. We cannot exist without that pleasure'*.

Apparently, the religion of the Jews was rejected because they had no homeland. Vladimir commented that they must have lost Jerusalem because God had abandoned them.

This left the religion of the Christians. But which form of Christianity: that of the Latin West, or Byzantine East? His emissaries reported that in the Latin German Church there was no beauty. But when his envoys arrived at Constantinople and witnessed the Divine Liturgy at the Hagia Sophia they exclaimed: *"We no longer knew whether we were in heaven or on earth."* Their reports of the magnificence of the Church, its heavenly music and the beauty of the icons convinced Vladimir that the Eastern Orthodox Byzantine rite would suit his people best. Furthermore, it was the tradition into which his Grandmother, Olga, had been baptised.

Vladimir was baptised in December 987 and took the Christian name Basil. His family and *boyars* (nobility) were then baptised. He ordered that all the wooden statues of the pagan gods be destroyed and the senior God, Perun, was flogged and thrown into the river. On the 1st August 988, he ordered the mass baptism in the river Dnieper of all the people of the Rus'.

From this moment missionaries and priests began arriving from Constantinople to train priests and educate the people in the Faith. Churches and schools were also built and the general level of education and culture rose significantly.

Vladimir's own baptism seems to have been sincere. According to the Chronicles, he released his many wives and concubines and remained faithful to Anna. He introduced the equivalent of a welfare state and reformed the penal system. From this point on Russia's relations with Constantinople and Eastern Orthodoxy were strengthened.

Conclusion

It is difficult to know the truth surrounding the early period of Russian history. Most of the written information we have comes from chronicles, which are usually commissioned and always written from one particular perspective. We do, however, have archeological evidence that Scandinavian people were present in Eastern Europe as traders from around the 6th Century.

The story that the Rus' were invited by the Finnic and Slavic tribes to come and rule over them may be questionable. It is evident, however that the leader of the Rus', was a chieftain named Rurik. It would also appear that in a fairly short period of time, the Rus' and the Slavs became integrated and the Varangian rulers adopted Slav names.

Exactly how the Rus' came to be converted to Christianity is also open to debate. The *Russian Primary Chronicle,* Byzantine, Muslim and Jewish accounts all vary. It is most likely that Vladimir believed that it would be politically expedient to unite his people under the power of one deity rather than a 'family of gods'. This had worked for the Roman Emperor Constantine in the 4th Century. Furthermore, the Rus' benefitted culturally and educationally by adopting Byzantine Orthodoxy.

Despite the speculation, it would appear that Vladimir's conversion was sincere. Certainly, his decision to adopt Eastern Orthodoxy, thereby tying the Kievan Rus' to Constantinople, was to have a profound effect on the future of the Russian people.

The importance of Vladimir in the history of Russia cannot be overestimated. However, the person Vladimir and the location of the conversion of the Rus' have become highly contested in recent times. Kiev is now the capital of an independent Ukraine and the Ukrainian people claim Volodymyr (Vladimir) as their own Saint. Russians also claim Vladimir as their own Saint, which is not surprising since the two countries share the same history. Indeed, it is this shared history that underlies much of the current tension between the two countries.

Ever since Russia annexed the Ukrainian region of Crimea in February 2014, tensions between the two countries have increased. In November 2016, President Putin added to this tension by unveiling a 16m statue of Vladimir the Great in front of the Kremlin in Moscow. Ukraine viewed this act as unnecessarily provocative.

*****

CHAPTER TWO

Wars and Invasions

Wars of Succession

Before Vladimir died in 1015, he divided his kingdom among his many sons. This marked the beginning of a system of inheritance known as *Appanage,* whereby the eldest of the royal princes, whether he be a brother, cousin, or uncle, became Grand Prince, rather than the eldest son. The Grand Prince traditionally ruled the city of Kiev, the 'Mother of Cities', while Novgorod, the first city to be settled by the Rus', was second in seniority and awarded to the next prince in line.

Appanage was originally practiced by the Slavs and was then adopted by the Varangian Rus', which is another example of how the Varangians became integrated into Slav tradition and culture. Unfortunately, the system usually led to conflict and wars of succession.

This was the case when Vladimir died in 1015. As the eldest son, Sviatopolk inherited the title of Grand Prince. But to ensure that there was no challenge to his position, he arranged the murder of his two of younger brothers, Boris and Gleb, who were later to become the first saints to be canonised as martyrs by the Russian Orthodox Church.

Having rid himself of any threat from his brothers, Sviatopolk then seized the city of Kiev with the help of his Polish wife's relatives. His rule was to be short-lived however. He was unpopular among the citizens, not only because of the brutal murder of his brothers, but also because of doubts over his paternity and therefore the legitimacy of his rule. He was ostensibly the son of the Greek nun who had been raped by his father. However, it was always possible that the child she bore was the son of her husband Yarapolk and not Vladimir. If this were the case, then Sviatopolk was not the son of Vladimir and would have no claim to the throne.

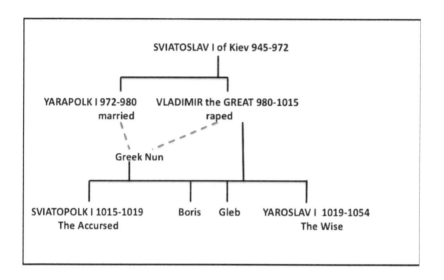

Yaroslav, a younger brother who was ruling Novgorod, decided to challenge Sviatopolk's right to rule as Grand Prince. He raised an army that included citizens of Novgorod and Varangian mercenaries and after several years of warfare he defeated Sviatopolk and took the city of Kiev. Yaroslav then rewarded the people of Novgorod by granting them special citizens' rights and privileges. This was a first step towards the later creation of an independent Novgorod Republic. After his defeat, Sviatopolk is thought to have fled to Poland to seek refuge with his in-laws. In 1019, Yaroslav became Grand Prince of Kiev and Novgorod.

Yaroslav the Wise: 1019-1054

During Yaroslav's long reign he increased his territories and forged alliances with foreign powers by arranging dynastic marriages for his ten children. One of his sons married the daughter of the Byzantine Emperor and a daughter was married to the Holy Roman Emperor Henry IV. Other children married into the royal families of France, Norway, Hungary and England.

Yaroslav constructed fortifications along the northeast boundary of his territory as protection against the constant threat of the Pechenegs and other Turkic tribes. He founded the city of Yaroslavi. He commissioned the Saint Sophia Cathedral in Kiev and the first Kievan monasteries of Saint George and Saint Irene. He built a school for the children of priests and declared 26th November as 'Yuri's Day', or Saint George's Day.

During his reign, the social divisions of society became more firmly established. The *Drujina*, an elite band of armed bodyguards or small personal army, had the highest status. Its members included soldiers, barons and *boyars* (aristocracy). Then, in descending order of importance, came the citizens, traders, the peasants and finally slaves.

But Yaroslav was also remembered for some more negative aspects, an example being when he imprisoned his youngest brother for life. Some chroniclers also suggest that it was he who arranged the murder of Boris and Gleb and not Sviatopolk who has been traditionally accused of the murder. Whatever the truth may be, Yaroslav, also known as the Lawgiver, has gone down in history as one of the greatest rulers of the Rus'.

Yaroslav's reign marked a watershed in the history of Kievan Rus. He broke with tradition in that he appointed a Slav monk, Hilarion, as Metropolitan of Kiev. Hilarion was a great scholar and author of *Sermon on Law and Grace,* which predated the *Primary Chronicle* and is thought to be one of the earliest pieces of literature of Kievan Rus'. Until Hilarion, all appointments had been made by Constantinople and only Greeks became bishops of the Rus. By appointing Hilarian, Yaroslav's intention was to make Kievan Rus' less dependent upon Byzantinium.

Probably Yarolsav's greatest achievement was the introduction of a new legal code known as the *Russkaya Pravda.* This, together with the many works of translation from Greek into Russian that he commissioned, earned him the title 'The Wise'.

The *Russkaya Pravda* reflected Slav and Varangian culture rather than Byzantine, which was another move on Yaroslav's part to distance the Rus' from Byzantium. For example, the barbaric punishments meted out by the Byzantines were originally alien to the Slav and were introduced to the Rus' largely through the influence of the Orthodox Church. Yaroslav's legislation was an attempt to redress the situation, very often by replacing corporal punishment with a system of fines. For example:

a) *If someone be beaten so that he bears bruises and is bloody, then he need seek no eyewitness [to confirm his complaint]; if he bears no sign [of the fight], then [let] an eyewitness come forward; if the [complainant] is unable [to produce a witness], then that is the end of the matter; if [the victim] is unable to avenge himself, then he is to take for the offense three grivnas, and also payment for the physician.*

b) *And for [killing] the prince's horse, if it is branded [the offender is to] pay three grivnas, and for a peasant's [horse he pays] two grivnas, for a mare 60 rezanas, for an ox one grivna, for a three-year-old [cow] 15 kunas, for a two-year-old [cow] one-half grivna, for a calf five rezanas, for a lamb one nogata, [and] for a ram one nogota.*

At that time, the cost of a horse would have been two *grivnas* and the cost of a serf, half a *grivna*. Fines payable for the death of, or bodily harm to, in the case of a woman was half that of a man. Trials by hot iron and water are also mentioned but this reflects the Norse, or Varangian tradition rather than Slav or Byzantine.

Yaroslav died in 1054, the year of the great schism between the Catholic Western Church of Rome and the Eastern Orthodox Church of Constantinople. His death marked the end of the 'Golden Age' of Kievan Rus'. Because he continued the tradition of *Appanage,* whereby his lands were divided up into numerous principalities among his male relatives, wars of succession were inevitable. Over the next hundred years instability and chaos prevailed leaving the Rus' weak and vulnerable to invasion.

Andrew Bogoliubski and the Fall of Kiev

By the middle of the 12th Century a powerful leader emerged in the Northern region. Prince Andrew Bogoluibski was Prince of Vladimir, Rostov and Suzdal and his great ambition was to unite all the Rus' by gaining the submission of Kiev and Novgorod. In 1167, he led a large army against Kiev. He virtually destroyed the city and seized the most precious religious artifacts including the Byzantine 'Mother of God' icon.

Andrew then made his younger brother, Gleb, Prince of the city but when Gleb died two years later the city was again fought over by different Rus' princes until it was finally conquered and destroyed by the Mongols in 1240.

Following his destruction of Kiev in 1167, Andrew moved the capital city of the Rus' to Vladimir, with himself as Grand Prince. He enlarged and fortified the city and commissioned the building of the Assumption Cathedral.

Novgorod Republic

Once established as Grand Prince at his new capital in Vladimir, Andrew's next ambition was to subdue Novgorod. But the opportunity escaped him. His authoritarian attitude made him unpopular with his *boyars*. He was assassinated in June 1174, before he could attempt an assault on the city.

Being located in the far northeast corner of Kievan Rus', Novgorod was geographically distanced from Constantinople and therefore Byzantine influence. Instead, it looked westwards across the Baltic Sea towards Scandinavia. The city, known as 'Lord Novgorod the Great' had always been fiercely independent and especially so from 1019, when Yaroslav the Wise had granted the citizens special rights and privileges.

Although in theory the Prince of Novgorod was appointed by the Grand Prince of Kiev, in practice, the *Veche,* or City Assembly, had the last word. According to the *Novgorod Chronicle*, the *Veche* frequently 'let go', or 'fetched away' an unwanted Prince, which was another way of saying 'we don't want you'. In such circumstances, the Prince would be wise to leave quickly.

In 1136, the Novgorodians rejected their Prince, Vsevolod Mstislavich, who had been nominated by the Grand Prince of Kiev. This act of independence marked the beginning of the Novgorod Republic, which was to last until 1478 when it became incorporated into the Grand Duchy of Moscow.

The Germans

From early times Novgorad had been an important trading post for goods travelling to and from Constantinople. By the middle of the 12th Century the city had become part of the Hanseatic League, which was a network of commercial cities containing warehouses and often fortifications to protect their mercantile. Normally the gates surrounding the Hanseatic area of the city were closed at night to protect both the merchants and their goods. Novgorod, along with London, was one of the main non-German cities of the League, whereas the majority were German cities located along the Baltic Coast and the Rivers Rhine and Danube.

Because of Novgorod's connection with the Hanseatic League, the city became home to many German merchants who lived in the commercial quarter of the city. Initially relations between the Novgorodians and the Germans were good, but things started to change towards the end of the 12th Century, that were directly related to the Crusades.

In 1188, Pope Gregory VIII proclaimed a third Crusade. The aim was to retake the holy city of Jerusalem after it had been recaptured in 1187 by Salah ad-Din Yusuf, known in the West as Saladin. This Crusade is also known as 'The Kings' Crusade' because it was led by the rulers of three major European powers; King Philip II of France, King Richard I of England, also known as 'The Lionheart' and Frederick Barbarossa, the Holy Roman Emperor.

Frederick Barbarossa, who was elderly at the time, never did reach the Holy Land. There is some debate as to how he actually died, but the general consensus is that he accidentally drowned in a shallow river in southern Anatolia. One theory is that whilst seeking relief in the water from the extreme heat, his heavy armour weighed him down causing him to drown.

The majority of the German troops returned home, while the remaining French and English troops continued towards Jerusalem. They failed to retake the holy city but they did succeed in capturing the coastal cities of Jaffa and Acre.

The crusaders remained in Acre for approximately another hundred years and it was during this time that the Order of Brothers of the German House of Saint Mary in Jerusalem, better known as the Teutonic Order, or Teutonic Knights, was formed. In common with the Knights Hospitaller, or Knights of St John of Jerusalem, the Teutonic Knights were founded in order to protect Christian pilgrims and establish hospitals.

In 1211, the Teutonic Knights moved to Transylvania to help defend the Hungarians against the Turkic Kipchaks and in 1230 they began a series of campaigns against the pagans of the Baltic States. The Teutonic Knights were not the first military monks crusading in the region however. Albert, Prince Bishop of Riga, began the conversion of pagan Livonians when he founded the Livonian Brothers of the Sword in 1202. The Order was sanctioned by Pope Innocent III and supported by the Holy Roman Emperor. In 1204, while Western Crusaders were sacking Constantinople during the Fourth Crusade, 1,500 knights of the Livonian Brothers of the Sword sailed in 23 vessels along the Baltic Coast on a mission intended to convert the pagan Balts.

In 1236 the Livonian Order merged with the Teutonic Knights. They acquired vast tracts of land, built fortresses and engaged in international trade. For over two hundred years, between 1200 and 1450, the State of the Teutonic Order ruled modern day Estonia, Latvia and Lithuania and parts of Poland and Russia.

The city 'Lord Novgorod the Great', the proud city of Kievan Rus', religious and cultural centre of Orthodox Christianity, was inevitably affected by the proximity of aggressive crusading knights on a mission to convert all Slavs, whether pagan or Orthodox, to Catholic Christianity. This dramatically changed the relationship between the German merchants living in Novgorod and the people of Novgorod.

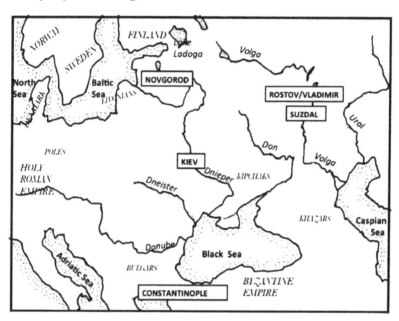

Alexander Nevsky

This was the situation when Alexander, second son of Prince Yaroslav II, became Grand Prince of Vladimir in 1252. He ranks alongside Rurik and Yaroslav the Wise as one of the greatest rulers of Kievan Rus'. But he is best known in Russian history for his defense of the Rus' against the Swedes and particularly the Germans, for which he was canonised in 1547.

According to the *Second Pskovian Chronicle*,

'He was taller than others and his voice reached the people as a trumpet, and his face was like the face of Joseph, whom the

Egyptian Pharaoh placed as next to the king after him of Egypt. His power was a part of the power of Samson and God gave him the wisdom of Solomon ...this Prince Alexander: he used to defeat but was never defeated.'

Alexander's first military challenge came when he was just 20 years. For centuries, the Swedes and the Rus' had competed for the region of Finland and particularly the Gulf of Finland. On the 15th July 1240, Swedish forces, together with their Prince and bishops, landed at the confluence of the rivers Izhora and Neva. Their aim was to seize Novgorod and Ladoga.

According to the *Chronicle of Novgorod, 'Alexander with the men of Novgorod and of Ladoga did not delay at all; he went against them and defeated them...And there was great slaughter of Svei* (Swedes). *And Knayaz* (Prince) *Alexander with the men of Novgorod and of Ladoga all came back in health to their own country.'*

Some doubt has been placed on the historical accuracy of this account because it is only mentioned in the Russian chronicles and not in any contemporary non-Russian source. Whatever the truth may be, from that time the Prince was known as Alexander Nevsky in reference to the River Neva.

Two years later, Alexander once more came to the aid of the Novgorodians. On the 5th April 1242, the Livonian Branch of the Teutonic Knights invaded the region of Lake Peipus that formed the border between the Republic of Novgorod and the Teutonic States. All accounts agree that a battle took place on the frozen ice of the lake and that the Novgorodians defeated the German knights. Historians differ however over the detail. For example, some suggest that the story of the ice cracking due to the weight of the armed knights and horses, first appeared in 1938 in Sergei Eisenstein's film *Alexander Nevsky.* Non-Russian sources claim that the Russian chroniclers inflated the figures for the number of German troops while stressing their own, much smaller, numbers. However, this is not a serious accusation since most historical documents are written from one perspective and should be read with a certain amount of skepticism.

The legacy of Alexander Nevsky in Russian history is immense. He was canonised as St Alexander Nevsky in 1547 with his principal feast day being 23rd November. In the 18th Century, Tsar Peter the Great ordered that his remains be removed from Vladimir and reinterred at the Alexander Nevsky Lavra, or monastery, in St. Petersburg.

In 1725, Empress Catherine I introduced the 'Imperial Order of St Alexander Nevsky' and in 1942 the Soviet authorities introduced an' Order of Alexander Nevsky'. Apart from the 1938 film *Alexander Nevsky*, Sergei Prokofiev, who wrote the soundtrack for the film, reworked part of the score into a well-known concert piece.

Alexander has justifiably been acclaimed as an ideal prince-soldier and defender of Russia for his campaigns in the West against the Swedes and Germans. His later actions in relation to invaders from the East, the Mongols, have not received universal acclaim.

Conclusion

The long reign of Yaroslav the wise, between 1019 and 1054, represented the Golden Age of Kievan Rus'. It was a time of cultural flowering, the building of many churches and monasteries and the foundation of schools. It was also a time when the Rus', or at least the leaders, started to become aware of their Russian sense of identity. Yaroslav's appointment of a Slav bishop, rather than accept a Greek bishop imposed by Constantinople, and his legal code, the *Russkaya Pravda*, were both overt attempts to distance the Rus' from Byzantium.

Following the destruction of Kiev in 1167 by Andrew Bogoliubski, the northern cities of Rostov, Suzdal and especially Vladimir assumed greater significance. This was especially the case when the Grand Prince chose to make a particular city his capital. However, while Kiev may have lost its political importance, it continued to be the centre of Christian Orthodoxy for the Kievan Rus'.

Events in the Near East and Holy Land that led to the Crusades were to have repercussions right across Europe as far as the Baltic coast. The zeal of the Northern Crusaders often led to a religious fanaticism that was directed not just against the pagan Slav, but also the Orthodox Christian. When the Teutonic Knights threatened the fiercely independent citizens of Novgorod, they were repelled under the leadership of Grand Prince Alexander Nevsky.

Alexander Nevsky has come to symbolise the victory of Russia over the Swedes and particularly the Germans. Down the centuries Russian soldiers have received military honours in his name. Films have been made and music composed with the aim of instilling pride in the Russian people and loyalty to the nation of Russia.

Lake Peipus, the site of the German defeat, became the border between Eastern Orthodoxy and Roman Catholicism. Three hundred years later, both the Swedes and Germans would challenge the authority of the Papacy and the institute of the Catholic Church at the time of the 16th Century Reformation.

*****

CHAPTER THREE

The Mongol Yoke

While Alexander Nevsky was fighting off the Swedes and German Teutonic Knights in the Northwest, another invasion was happening in the East. According to the *Chronicle of Novgorod*, *'unknown nations arrived. No one knew their origin or whence they came, or what religion they practiced. This is known only to God, and perhaps to wise men learned in books'.*

The Mongols who invaded Kievan Rus' were known as the Golden Horde, or the Ulus of Jochi. There have been various theories put forward regarding the name 'Golden Horde', the most popular being that 'Golden' referred to the gold coloured tent of Batu Khan or perhaps the wealth that the Mongols accumulated. 'Horde' may have been related to the Mongol word for 'camp', or 'centre'.

The Golden Horde appeared in 1223 and for most the next two hundred years the Rus' people lived under Mongol vassalage. The Horde's success in conquering and subduing the Rus' principalities is largely due to the on-going infighting among the Rus' Princes. This created a political vacuum leaving them open to assault from an outside enemy. Since the Mongol invasion marks the end of Kievan Rus' polity, the nation and the people will now be referred to as Russia and the Russians respectively.

Russians themselves refer to the period from 1223 to 1480 as the Mongol Yoke, suggesting that the people suffered a terrible burden. Alternative views are that there was never a Mongol 'yoke' or that the benefits introduced by the Mongols outweighed the negative aspects.

The Mongols

The founder of the Mongol Empire, Genghis Khan, was born around 1162 in the Kentii Mountains of Mongolia. By 1206 he had succeeded in uniting under his leadership the many nomadic Mongol tribes and consequently earned the title 'Great Khan', better known in the West as Genghis Khan. Genghis was a brilliant, though brutal, military leader as well as being an astute strategist. Under threat of punishment, he demanded absolute loyalty from both his own people and also his vassal states. By the end of the 13th Century the Empire that he founded stretched from the Black Sea to China, bringing him a source of great wealth and power.

Before Genghis Khan died in 1227, he divided his territories between his four senior sons. There was some doubt about the paternity of his eldest son, Jochi. A rival tribe had held Genghis Khan's young wife captive for a short while and it was always possible that the child she gave birth to was fathered by that tribal leader and not by Genghis. The situation was similar to that of Sviatopolk, who may, or may not, have been the son of Vladimir, a situation that resulted in conflict with his brother Yaroslav. (See Chapter Two)

Genghis, however, wisely decided not to pass on the title of Great Khan to Jochi. Instead he appointed his third son Ogedei, who was also the most able, as Great Khan. Then he divided the entire Empire between his four senior sons. Jochi was given the Western part of the Empire that included the region of the Caucasus and parts of today's Russia. Chagatai received Central Asia and Northern Iran. Ogedei received Eastern Asia and China while the youngest son, Tolui, was given the Mongol homeland, roughly equating to present day Mongolia. In relation to Russian history, which is the topic of this book, we are interested in Jochi's inheritance.

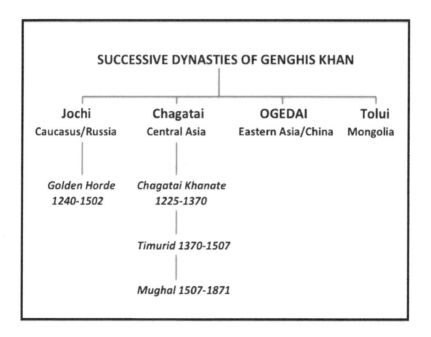

SUCCESSIVE DYNASTIES OF GENGHIS KHAN

Jochi	Chagatai	OGEDAI	Tolui
Caucasus/Russia	Central Asia	Eastern Asia/China	Mongolia

Golden Horde
1240-1502

Chagatai Khanate
1225-1370

Timurid 1370-1507

Mughal 1507-1871

Jochi's troops, under the leadership of Generals Jeb and Subutai the Valiant, first engaged with the Russians in May 1223 at the Battle of Kalka River, which is in the Southeastern region of today's Ukraine. The Russian army consisted of a coalition of principalities led by Mstislav III, Grand Prince of Kiev, as well as the Turkic Cumans. The Cumans, Kipchaks and Penechegs were all Turkic tribes who had migrated from the East over previous centuries and settled in the Northern region of the Black Sea. At various times, they had been at war both with the Rus' and the Byzantines. However, when faced with a common enemy, in this case the Mongols, the Cumans decided to ally with the Russian princes. Furthermore, it was the Cumans who first warned the Russians of the danger of the advancing Mongols.

Although the Mongols defeated the Russians in the first battle of 1223, they decided to retreat, probably because the Great Khan needed reinforcements in his ongoing war with the Chinese Jin. It would be another thirteen years before the Mongols returned, this time under the leadership of Batu Khan, the son of Jochi and grandson of Genghis Khan.

Invasions of Batu Khan

Having finally defeated the Jin in 1234, the Great Khan Ogedei now turned his attention to the West. He ordered his nephew Batu to commence the conquest of Europe. In 1235, accompanied by his cousins Mongke and Guyuk, Batu led an army of mounted archers across the Volga River. Estimates of troop numbers vary widely from 30,000 to 200,000 and over the next twelve months the Mongols defeated the Volga Bulgarians, the Kipchak Cumans and the Alans, an ancient Iranian nomadic people, who had earlier settled in the region.

In 1237, Batu sent an envoy to Yuri II, Grand Prince of Vladimir, offering him a choice between submission or war. Yuri had the envoy murdered and refused to submit. He also refused to go to the help of Ryazan, which was under siege from the Mongols at the time. Consequently, Batu sacked Ryazan and then went on to destroy Kolomna and Moscow, which at that time was a fairly insignificant town. He next advanced on the capital city of Vladimir and burned it to the ground. The Grand Prince managed to escape to Yaroslavi, but his wife and all his family died in a fire that raged through the cathedral where they were hiding.

In 1238, Batu divided his armies into smaller contingents in order to take the smaller cities. Crimea and Mordovia fell with many of the Cumans and Greeks of Crimea escaping to the Crimean Mountains. In time, the refugees integrated with the Mongols and became known as the Crimean Tatars.

Rostov, Yaroslavi and Tver fell in the same year. In the winter of 1239, Batu sacked Chernigov and Peryaslavi and in the winter of 1240, Kiev, the great city of Vladimir the Great and Kievan Rus', was completely destroyed. Only Novgorod and Pskov survived unscathed.

Batu then began making plans to conquer Austria, Italy and Germany. While no Western powers came to the help of the Russians when they were under attack from the Mongols, as soon as the territory of the Holy Roman Empire was in danger, Emperor Frederick II and Pope Gregory IX decided to call a crusade to defeat the pagan invaders. However, there was very little response from the monarchs of Western Europe who were all caught up at the time in their own affairs.

Everything changed, however, with the death of the Great Khan, Ogedei, in December 1241. Under Mongol, or *Yasa* Law, all Khans of the dynasty were expected to return to Mongolia on the death of the Great Khan. At a special *Kurultai*, or grand council, held in the capital city of Karakorum, they would then elect their new leader.

It took five years to find a successor to Ogedei. The long interval was partly because Batu refused to return home and sent a deputy instead. But the delay was also caused by the vast distances involved. For example, it could take up to three years at that time to travel from Russia to Mongolia. During the interregnum, Toregene, Ogedei's wife became regent as the Great Khatun. She ruled until 1246, when Batu's cousin Guyuk Khan, who had accompanied Batu on his conquests, was elected Great Khan.

As was customary, Toregen invited rulers of other great Empires, including the Sultans of the Seljuk and Abbasid Empires, to the coronation ceremony. Yaroslav, Grand Prince of Vladimir and Suzdal, was also invited to the ceremony but he died under suspicious circumstances, thought to be from poisoning at the hands of Toregen.

The death of Ogedei and consequent recall of Batu to Mongolia disrupted any further conquests of Russian territory and saved Western Europe from the Mongol Yoke. It did not, however, lead to the departure of the Mongols. Instead, there began a period of consolidation under their rule.

The Yoke

The Mongol conquest caused untold devastation to Russian cities, property and land, resulting in economic decline. It is estimated that around half a million Russians lost their lives between 1223 and 1246. Once the initial conquest was over, Batu introduced new forms of administration, some of which had originated in China.

The Mongol 'yoke' primarily consisted of homage, tribute in the form of taxation and a troop levy. Once a city was conquered, either by force or through submission, the Prince was expected to pay personal homage to his overlord. Initially this meant a long and arduous journey to Mongolia. It was a journey that could take many years and some Princes were known to have died on the way.

Having arrived at the Mongolian capital, the Grand Prince had to prostrate at the feet of the Great Khan. This would have been a humiliating experience for the Princes of the proud house of Rurik. The prince would then be awarded a *yarlyk*, which was a legal document granting him authority to rule his domain. Later, when the Golden Horde established its capital at Sarai, which borders the Caspian Sea in the region of modern Astrakan in Russia, the journey was far less demanding. As vassals of the Golden Horde, all successive Princes could only rule after paying personal homage to the Khan and receiving the required *yarlyk* and in many cases the Khan appointed his own Prince, overriding the wishes of the people.

Taxation

In order to collect tribute in the form of taxation, the Mongols needed to know the size of the population. In 1257 they conducted a census, using a Chinese system whereby the population was divided into multiples of ten. This was several centuries before similar exercises were to be conducted in Europe.

Governors were then appointed with the responsibility of administering the area and collecting taxes. If a city had resisted the Mongols it was put under the jurisdiction of a military governor. But when a city surrendered it was placed under the authority of a civilian governor. In time, Russians were appointed as governors.

With the appointment of governors, the Mongols abolished the traditional *veche,* or council. This was a significant change and marked the dismantling of the traditional Slav democratic form of self-government and a move towards more autocratic rule that was to culminate in the autocracy of imperial Russia.

Novgorod, Pskov and several other cities in the Northwestern region, managed to keep their *veche*. This is partly because the Mongols were less interested in these far-flung regions. Furthermore, Novgorod was at the time ruled by Grand Prince Alexander Nevsky (see previous Chapter) and rather than have his city razed to the ground, he chose to submit to Batu, an act that drew fierce criticism from many of his people. However, by submitting to the Mongols, Alexander was able to keep his *veche* and be accountable to a civilian, rather than a military governor. Furthermore, Alexander frequently acted as an intermediary between the Russians and the Khan, particularly in cases where the Khan was on the point of taking punitive action against a principality.

According to Dustin Hosseini, in his article *The Effects of the Mongol Empire on Russia,* published by the School of Russian and Asian Studies, the spirit of the *veche,* as a public forum for debate, is witnessing resurgence in Russia today.

Troop and other Levies

The census statistics were also used to set the amount of troop levy demanded by the overlords. According to the number of inhabitants, all towns and villages were expected to provide a certain number of troops to fight alongside the Mongols in their campaigns.

Apart from troops, the Russian population also had to provide *yams*, or staging posts. The posts were spread across Mongol Russia, each separated by a distance of a day's horse ride. The *yams* offered fresh horses, food and bedding to troops and Mongol agents, all of which had to be provided by the local people. While the posts enabled travel across vast distances, they did not incorporate a postal service.

The Russian Orthodox Church

When Batu and the Golden Horde invaded Russia in the 13th Century, the Mongols were still following the religion of Genghis Khan, which was a mixture of Tengrism, or ancestor worship and shamanism. They were known to be tolerant of other religions, including Christianity. Despite this, at the beginning of the invasion, churches were looted and priests killed alongside the rest of the population.

However, Batu soon recognised the influence that the Church had over the people and decided to harness this influence, or power, for his own ends. In other words, his aim was to seek the collaboration of the Church to help him rule the people. He therefore needed to win the support of the Church hierarchy.

He first of all exempted the Church from the census programme. This naturally resulted in an exemption of all taxation and troop levy obligations. And in order to ensure that this was adhered to, he passed a decree declaring that: '*We don't require the church to pay any tribute, nor any tax per plough, nor any duty, nor provide horses, nor recruits, nor food supplies...*' (Alexander Yanov in his article *The Russian Orthodox Church and the Curse of the Mongol Yoke*, published by the Institute of Modern Russia).

But the act that was to have the most profound consequences was the award of a special *yarlyk*. According to Alexander Yanov, the Mongol khan issued a decree permitting the Church to seize over a third of all agricultural land in the country. Another edict stated: '*Let it* [the Church] *have the power to investigate the truth and to administer justice and to rule over its own people in all matters concerning robberies, theft, and all other cases, let it be decided by the Metropolitan himself, alone, or whomever he directs to do so*'.

The church benefitted hugely under the Mongol 'yoke'. In return for favours received, the Metropolitan ordered that prayers should be said for the Mongol Tsar, the legitimate ruler, who should be respected and obeyed in all things.

Apart from growing in wealth and power, compared to the rest of the Russian population, the Church experienced a flourishing in missionary work, church building and religious art.

It was during this period that the icon painter, Theophanes the Greek, moved from Constantinople, first to Novgorod and then to Moscow. The artist was commissioned to decorate churches and cathedrals with some of the greatest pieces of religious art. Theophanes was mentor and teacher to Andrei Rublev, who later painted icons and frescoes for the Cathedral of the Annunciation of the Moscow Kremlin. By 1322, Moscow had replaced first Kiev and then Vladimir as the Metropolitan (Church) capital.

There was also a growth at this time in the foundation of monasteries. With the collapse of Kievan Rus' and consequent political vacuum, large numbers flocked to the protection offered by the Church. In response monasteries were founded on agricultural land previously seized from the people. While a minority of Russians would have followed the religious life, the majority worked the land as unpaid labour.

Conclusion

The Mongol invasion of the Rus' was part of Genghis Khan's massive conquest of vast swathes of Central Asia and the Caucasus. Under the Great Khan's grandson, Batu, who led the Golden Horde, Kievan Rus' was conquered and came under Mongol vassalage for some two hundred years. This could not have happened in the way that it did without the anarchy that prevailed at the time among the Rus' principalities. In other words, a power gap had been created due to the infighting among the Princes. It was a gap into which the Mongols stepped.

Initially the conquest was less about acquiring land and more about the acquisition of wealth, primarily through taxation. This required an efficient form of administration and in order to achieve this Batu introduced a number of Chinese methods of recording. At the same time, he abolished the majority of the *veche,* or city councils, replacing them with military or civilian Governors. Finally, he succeeded in winning over the loyalty of the Church, which became a useful Mongol agent.

The overall effect of the Khan's strategy was to undermine the traditional democratic system of the Rus' while moving towards a more centralised form of government. It was a trend that was to continue into modern times.

There has been much debate over the nature of the 'yoke', if indeed, it ever existed. As so often happens, historians label a particular period long after the event. In this case, the first mention of a 'yoke' appeared in a late 17th Century Church school textbook when it described Ivan III's liberation of Muscovy Russia from the Horde 'yoke' in 1502.

It is unquestionable that the Mongol invasion caused destruction and human suffering, together with huge economic problems, on a vast scale. At the same time the Church, under the protection of the Mongols, witnessed a growth in wealth and power. It acquired agricultural land and built new Churches and monasteries, which were decorated by the greatest artists of the time.

During two hundred years of Mongol rule there was inevitably a degree of integration between Slav, Varangian and Mongol. Mongol words began to seep into the Russian language, the Russian elite started to wear Mongol dress and of course inter-racial marriage became commonplace. Indeed, it is possible to detect Mongol features in a large number of today's Russian population.

Whether or not the Mongol 'yoke' was a good, or bad, thing for Russia will long be debated. Some view the period to be the golden age of the Church. Others suggest that the 'yoke' was the cause of Russia's backwardness and orientalism that resulted in Russia falling behind the rest of Western Europe.

What is clear, however, is that the Mongol 'yoke' was a watershed in Russian history. It marked the end of Kievan Rus' and a move towards autocracy. It also enabled the rise of Muscovy, which will be the topic of the following Chapter.

*****

CHAPTER FOUR
Grand Duchy of Muscovy

The Grand Duchy of Muscovy, also known as Moscow, lasted from 1283 to 1503. In 1237, when conquered by the Mongols, the Duchy was an insignificant town within the Grand Principality of Vladimir Suzdal. By 1503, under the reign of Ivan III, known as the Great, Muscovy had tripled in size to incorporate all the previous territory of Kievan Rus'.

Daniel I, First Duke of Moscovy

In 1283, Daniel, the fourth and youngest son of Alexander Nevsky, inherited the minor principality. Located in an isolated region amongst thick forests, it was of little interest to the Mongols after their earlier sack of the city. It did, however, have the benefit of easy access to a number of important rivers that enabled trade with the Baltic and Constantinople.

Within ten years of Daniel's accession, he had absorbed Ryazan into his principality and he also succeeded in defeating an alliance of Pereslavi-Zalessky and the Mongols. Although not a large battle in terms of numbers, it was significant as being the earliest successful challenge to Mongol rule and it also brought Pereslavi into Daniel's domain. His conflict with Pereslavi was his only war during his thirty years' rule, which is recorded as being a period of relative peace.

During his reign, Daniel built the first monastery in Moscow, now known as the Danilov Monastery. He is said to have been a man of humility and he became a monk towards the end of his life. In 1652, Daniel was canonised by the Russian Orthodox Church.

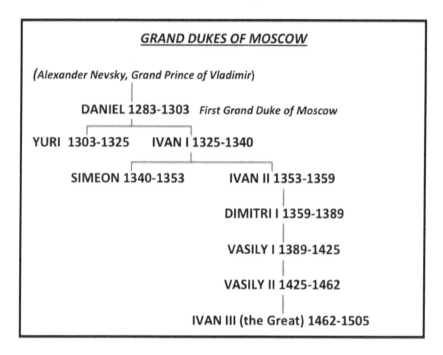

GRAND DUKES OF MOSCOW

(Alexander Nevsky, Grand Prince of Vladimir)

DANIEL 1283-1303   *First Grand Duke of Moscow*

YURI 1303-1325   IVAN I 1325-1340

SIMEON 1340-1353   IVAN II 1353-1359

DIMITRI I 1359-1389

VASILY I 1389-1425

VASILY II 1425-1462

IVAN III (the Great) 1462-1505

Yuri, Grand Duke of Moscovy 1303-1325

Yuri, Daniel's eldest son, who was also known as Georgiy, succeeded his father as Grand Duke in 1303. While Daniel had been a popular Grand Duke, who had introduced a period of relative peace and stability, this was not the case with Yuri.

Although Daniel had resisted going to war during his reign, this did not mean that he had no enemies, particularly when Moscow began to eclipse some of the other principalities. Yuri's first challenge came from Mikhail, who was a younger brother of Alexander Nevsky. As Prince of Tver and Grand Prince of Vladimir, Mikhail claimed Yuri's territories of Pereslavi and Moscow. Being the legitimate Grand Prince of Vladimir, Mikhail appealed to Great Khan Tokhta for support. In response, the Khan reaffirmed Mikhail as supreme ruler of the Russian princes, which by definition put Yuri in a subordinate position.

Yuri therefore looked elsewhere for support and he chose the Church, which was a rising power at the time. (See previous

44

Chapter) It was known that Metropolitan Peter, head of the Church, had a poor relationship with Mikhail of Tver ever since 1308, when the latter openly opposed Peter's candidature for the Episcopacy, even though it had been proposed by Constantinople. Taking advantage of the situation, Yuri gained the support of Metropolitan Peter in order to form an alliance with Novgorod against Mikhail of Tver.

When the Great Khan Tokhta died in 1313, both Yuri and Mikhail travelled to Sarai for the installation of his successor, Uzbeg Khan. Both Grand Princes spent some two to three years in the Mongol capital and during this time Yuri managed to win the favour of Uzbeg and married his sister Konchaka. Uzbeg then deposed Mikhail in favour of Yuri as Grand Prince of Vladimir and Yuri marched on Tver in order to claim his position as legitimate ruler. However, he was attacked by Mikhail's troops and his wife and brother were taken prisoner.

Konchaka died while being held hostage in Tver and Yuri reported to the Khan that Mikhail had poisoned his sister. Consequently, Mikhail was summoned to Sarai where he was put on trial, found guilty and promptly executed.

Yuri was not a popular ruler. The Khan had appointed him as tax-gatherer responsible for all the Russian people and consequently he acquired great wealth. He was also suspected of withholding tribute that was due to the Khan. When Mikhail's son and successor Dmitri, told Uzbeg Khan of his suspicions, both Yuri and Dmitri were summoned to Sarai. But before any investigation could take place, Dmitri arranged the murder of Yuri. Dmitri was executed by the Horde some months later.

Ivan I, Grand Duke of Moscovy 1325-1340

Following Yuri's death in 1325, he was succeeded by his younger brother Ivan I as Grand Duke of Moscovy. Three years later, Uzbeg Khan awarded him the senior principality of Vladimir along with the right to collect taxes from all the other Russian principalities. Following in the footsteps of his brother, Ivan also became very wealthy and earned the nickname *Kalita*, meaning 'money-bag'.

During Ivan's rule, the Grand Duchy of Muscovy increased both in terms of territory and population. With increased wealth Ivan was able to loan money to poorer principalities, many of which fell into deep debt. As they became increasingly dependent upon the Grand Duke, they were vulnerable to annexation by Moscow. Ivan also bought land from poor farmers in the area around the city, which further increased the territory of Muscovy.

The population of Moscow grew partly because of an influx of refugees from less stable areas. Added to this, Ivan adopted a policy of paying ransoms to the Horde for the release of Russian prisoners taken in Mongol raids. On release, these prisoners were forced to settle in Moscow.

As a sign of the growing importance of the city, Metropolitan Peter, head of the Russian Orthodox Church, decided to move from Vladimir to Moscow. Although the Metropolitan's residence became Moscow, his title remained Metropolitan of Kiev and all Rus'. During Ivan's reign, he commissioned the building of the first stone churches in Moscow such as the original Assumption Cathedral. He also established his residence on Borovitsky Hill, the site of today's Kremlin.

Uzbeg Khan, Great Khan of the Golden Horde 1313-1341

Uzbeg, sometimes spelt Oz Beg, was the Great Khan of the Golden Horde during the reign of Ivan I and it was Uzbeg who awarded Ivan the Grand Dukedom of Muscovy. Uzbeg was the first Khan of the Horde to become a Muslim, all previous Khans following the animist and shamanist religion of the Mongols. Uzbeg was also the longest reigning of all Khans and during his rule the territory of the Golden Horde reached its zenith.

Uzbeg imposed Islam on all Mongols living within the territories of the Golden Horde and all subsequent Great Khans were Muslim. However, he remained tolerant towards people of other religions, which is exemplified by the following letter written to Metropolitan Peter:

By the will and power, the greatness and most high! Let no man insult the metropolitan church of which Peter is head, or his service or his churchman; let no man seize their property, goods or people, let no man meddle in the affairs of the church...Their laws, their churches and monasteries and chapels shall be respected; whoever condemns or blames this religion, shall not be allowed to excuse himself under any pretext, but shall be punished with death. (*The Preaching of Islam: A History of the Propagation of the Muslim Faith* by Sir Thomas Walker Arnold)

Uzbeg also had good relations with the Latin Pope, probably because he permitted the building of Catholic Churches for use by the Genoese and Venetians traders who he allowed to settle in the Crimea.

The Mongol capital of Sarai prospered under Uzbeg. To cater for the growing Muslim adherents, mosques were built on a grand scale as well as baths, caravanserai and government buildings. Trade flourished, attracting merchants from the Islamic countries of the region as well as from Europe and Asia. The new Mongol city, which under Uzbeg became known as 'New Sarai', was also a centre for trade in European slaves, mainly with the Mamluk Empire of Egypt, with whom Uzbeg was on good terms.

Vasili II, Grand Duke of Muscovy, 1425-1462

Between the death of Ivan I in 1342 and the reign of Vasili II in 1425, four different Grand Dukes ruled over Muscovy. When Vasili II came to the throne it was the beginning of a period of great upheaval for Muscovy. The early years were marred by internecine struggle for the title of Grand Duke, which led to the first civil war in the history of Muscovy. Until that time Muscovy had enjoyed relative peace and steady growth.

Vasili II was only ten when he inherited the title from his father Vasili I, while his mother assumed the role of Regent. However, his uncle Yuri of Zvenigorod, together with his two sons Vasili, known as the Cross-Eyed and Dmitri Shemyaka, challenged Vasili II on the grounds that his accession was against the Rus' tradition of *appanage*, whereby succession went to the eldest male relative rather than the eldest son. Both sides appealed to the Great Khan for arbitration. To add to the conflict, the Khan swapped his support from one party to another. This practice was frequently used by Great Khans of the Horde in their policy of 'divide and rule'.

In the early years of the conflict, Vasili was imprisoned and blinded by his cousin Dmitri. Thereafter he became known as Vasili the Blind.

Conflict within the Church

Apart from instability resulting from civil war, Vasili II also ruled at a time of crisis for the Orthodox Church. The catalyst for the crisis was the increasing threat from the Ottoman Empire. For over a century, the Ottoman Turks had been making inroads into Byzantine territory and by the end of the 14th Century, Constantinople was virtually an island surrounded by a sea of Islam. It was just a question of time before the city fell to the Turks, unless the Christian West came to her aid.

Relations between the Eastern Orthodox Church and the Western Latin Church had broken down in 1054 over political and theological issues, resulting in a schism. Then the situation was made even worse in 1204, during the Fourth Crusade, when Western Crusaders sacked Constantinople and the Pope installed a Latin Patriarch to rule over the Orthodox faithful.

Despite this, the Byzantine Emperor, John VIII Palaiologos, decided to appeal to Pope Eugene IV in Rome for help in defending Constantinople from the Turks. The Pope agreed, but only on condition that the Eastern and Western Churches be united under the supremacy of the Papacy. In order to save Constantinople, John Palaiologos agreed to the unification.

The Patriarch of Constantinople appointed Isadore, a Greek bishop, as Metropolitan of Kiev and All Rus' to oversee the process of unification. Isadore was renowned for his pro-Union stance as well his scholarship and oratory skills. From the beginning, his appointment was unpopular among many Rus' bishops as well as Grand Duke Vasili II.

In 1438, Isadore and Palaiologos led a delegation, including the

Patriarch of Constantinople and representatives of the Patriarchal Sees of Antioch and Alexandria, to Ferrara where initial discussions began under the chairmanship of the Pope. The delegation later moved to Florence and in July 1439, at the Council of Florence, agreement to the Unification was reached.

At the same time, the Pope made Isadore a Cardinal of the Latin Church and also appointed him as Papal Legate for Lithuania, Livonia and All Rus'. This angered the Eastern bishops and for a short while, in 1440, Isadore was imprisoned under the charge of heresy.

Despite much opposition from many within the Orthodox Church, Isidore officially proclaimed the Union of the Eastern and Western Churches on the 12th December 1452. But it was too late to save the city. Constantinople fell to the Ottoman Turks on the 29th May 1453. Although the Union had been signed at the Council of Florence, the Eastern Orthodox Church has never accepted its validity.

Isadore was in Constantinople at the time of the siege by the Ottomans. In order to escape capture, he dressed a dead body in his ecclesiastical robes hoping that people would be fooled into thinking he was dead. While this saved his life, he did not escape capture. He was taken as a slave by the Turks but eventually managed to escape to Rome where the Pope appointed him Latin Patriarch of Constantinople and Archbishop of Cyprus.

Isadore's appointment as Metropolitan of Kiev and All Rus' in 1438, led to a period of turmoil, leaving the Orthodox Church virtually leaderless. Consequently, in 1448 the Council of Russian Bishops appointed Jonas, a Russian, as Metropolitan of Kiev and All Rus', without the consent of the Patriarch in Constantinople. By so doing, the Russian Church was declaring its independence from Constantinople, otherwise known as autocephaly.

Following the fall of Constantinople, the Moscow Patriarchate saw itself its legitimate successor to Byzantium. From here developed the 'Third Rome' theory: imperial Rome (first Rome) being succeeded by Constantinople (second Rome) and Constantinople being succeeded by Moscow (third Rome). When Ivan IV assumed the title of Tsar, meaning Caesar, in 1547, he saw himself as the legitimate successor to Caesar Augustus of the Roman Empire.

With the fall of the Byzantine Empire in 1453, Moscow became the spiritual centre of the Orthodox Church. At the same time, Byzantine scholars, artists and writers fled to Moscow in order to escape the Turks. Consequently, by the end of the 16th Century, Moscow's status as a cultural centre equaled that of many Western European cities.

Ivan III: Grand Duke of Muscovy, 1462-1505

Ivan III, the eldest son of Vasili II, succeeded as Grand Duke in 1462. His long rule, of almost forty years, is a watershed in Russian history. He is often referred to as the 'gatherer of the Rus' lands' because he brought the many independent duchies and principalities under the direct control of Moscow and he ended the system of *appanage*.

Crucially, he succeeded in bringing the independent-minded Novgorod into his orbit of power. From the early centuries of Russian history, Novgorod's relationship with the Baltic States had been strong. By the 15th Century, Novgorod had also formed close ties with Catholic Lithuania and as Moscow's power continued to grow, Novgorod turned to Lithuania for protection against Muscovy.

Ivan III viewed this as an act of betrayal against the Rus' and the Orthodox religion. He sent his armies into battle with the Novgorodians whom he defeated in 1471. Novgorod was forced to sue for peace and end her alliance with Lithuania. Apart from ceding vast tracts of land to Moscow, Novgorod also had to pay a large war indemnity.

During the next fifteen years, either by conquest, purchase, or marriage contract, Ivan brought the principalities of Varoslavi, Rostov, Tver and Vyatka, plus many minor principalities, under the authority of Moscow. By the end of his reign he had tripled the size of Muscovy. He also decreed that when Dukes and Princes died, their domains should pass to the Grand Duke in Moscow. In this way, he not only ended the system of *appanage*, but he also reduced the power of the aristocracy while at the same time moving further towards autocracy.

Sophia Palaiologos

Meanwhile, the Pope still had hopes of uniting with Moscow in a joint effort to stop the advance of the Ottoman Turks. His opportunity came when Ivan's first wife, Maria of Tver died in 1467. Taking advantage of the situation, the Pope proposed a marriage between Ivan and Zoe Palaiologos, niece of Constantine Palaiologos, the last Byzantine Emperor.

When the Ottomans sacked Constantinople in 1453, Zoe and her siblings were taken to Rome where they came under the care of the Pope who treated them extremely well. During her time in Rome, she came under the influence of the Catholic Church and took the name Sophia. By uniting the Grand Duke of Muscovy in marriage with Sophia, the Pope hoped to bring the Orthodox East and Catholic West together in an alliance.

After three years of negotiation, in 1472, the couple finally married. But the Pope was to be disappointed because immediately upon her arrival in Russia, Sophia returned to the faith of her ancestors. Whether this was due to pressure from her new husband, who was vehemently anti-Catholic, or from her own volition, is not clear.

What is clear, however, is that she had a strong influence, both on her husband and court life at Moscow. She refused to follow the normal practice whereby royal and aristocratic women lived in separate quarters. Instead she took an active role in public life and frequently met foreign dignitaries and ambassadors. Furthermore, under her influence, Byzantine court ceremonial was introduced into the Moscow court and around this time Ivan began using the title Tsar.

Decline of the Golden Horde

The Golden Horde was at its height during the reign of Uzbeg in 14th Century. From that time on, however, Mongol power went into steady decline, largely because of internal conflict. This was exacerbated when Tamurlaine, Amir of the Timurid Empire, marched across Central Asia at the end of the 14th Century. The Mongol khanates in his path were either destroyed or subjugated. Sarai, capital of the Golden Horde was also affected. The Great Khan began to lose his authority and the Horde started to split into small khanates.

In 1476, encouraged by Sophia, Ivan withheld the customary tribute to Sarai. The Great Khan Ahmed responded by sending an army to confront Ivan. Two battles ensued but on both occasions the Mongols were defeated. This essentially marked the end of the Mongol Yoke. Crimea, with whom Ivan had good relations, remained an important Khanate. Despite the fall of the Horde, Ivan maintained good relations with other Muslim powers as well as with the Ottomans.

Conclusion

The Grand Duchy of Moscow, or Muscovy, which lasted from 1283 to 1503, marked a bridge between the Slav dominated period of Kievan Rus' and the rise of Russia as an autocratic state under the rule of a Tsar. Under nine successive Grand Dukes, the status of Moscow changed from being an insignificant backwater town, to an important religious and cultural city on a par with many in the West.

Under Ivan III, the age-old tradition of *appanage* was abolished, being replaced by the inheritance of Muscovy going to the eldest son. As a result, the dynasty, which was still Rurik, became more autocratic and powerful.

Moscow's success can be attributed to several causes. The first Grand Duke, Daniel, won the support both of the Church and the Great Khan. Both alliances brought benefits but perhaps the greatest was the appointment of the Grand Duke of Muscovy as tax collector over all the Russian people. In this way, the Dukedom became extremely wealthy and with wealth came power.

Moscow also benefited from the fall of Constantinople in 1453 to the Turks. The city became the heir to Constantinople as the spiritual centre for Orthodoxy and Moscow also benefitted from an influx of Byzantine scholars and artists.

Attempts were made to bring the Orthodox and Catholic Churches together to fight off the Ottoman Turks, but all attempts made by the Pope were thwarted, largely because of the anti-Catholic feelings of many Orthodox bishops and lay people. These were feelings that could be traced back to the Sack of Constantinople by the Western crusaders in 1204.

Lastly, and perhaps most importantly, Ivan III is remembered for having freed the Russian people from the 'Mongol Yoke' and for this he earned the title 'Ivan the Great'. His namesake, Ivan IV, who will be the topic of the following Chapter, earned another title, 'Ivan the Terrible'.

*****

CHAPTER FIVE

Ivan IV, the Terrible

In 1505, Vasili III succeeded his father, Ivan III, as ruler of Muscovy. During his rule of almost thirty years, Vasili continued the policies of his father in bringing autonomous principalities under Muscovy and developing relations with foreign powers. In 1521, for example, he received an embassy from Ismail I, Shah of the Persian Safavid Empire. At the time, the Shah had hopes of forming an alliance with Russia against the Ottomans. However, Moscow's policy was to maintain good relations with the Sultan in order to protect Russian merchants trading in Ottoman territory.

Relations with Poland-Lithuania in the West continued to be difficult, largely over the issue of religion and fears of Catholic ambitions in Russian territory. Along the Eastern border sporadic invasions from various Tartar clans caused instability in the region.

Vasili also inherited from his father on-going tensions with the Russian Orthodox Church. Apart from conflicts with Rome, referred to in the previous Chapter, there were internecine problems between the Church, the *boyars* and the Grand Duke, who now styled himself Tsar.

For over two hundred years, the Church had benefitted under the Mongol Yoke at the expense of the nobility and the people. Under the patronage of the Great Khan, it had acquired vast tracts of land, property and peasant labour. Its monasteries had also benefitted through being exempt from both tax and the soldier levy.

With the fall of the Mongols and rise of Muscovy, Ivan III decided that the privileges awarded the Church should be curbed. He particularly wanted to break the hold that the monasteries had over the peasants, who were treated as slaves. In his *Sudebnik* (Law Code) of 1497, Ivan introduced a provision whereby peasants were permitted to leave their landowning masters, including the monasteries, on one day of the year: 26th November, known as *Yuri's* Day, or George's Day.

Possessors and Non-Possessors

During the same period, dissatisfaction was growing among some monks who believed that the Church and monasteries, with their great wealth and power, had strayed from the message of the early Church. An increasing number of such monks came under the influence of Nil Sorsky (c 1433-1508), a monk born into the nobility, well-educated and widely travelled. Crucially, Sorsky had spent some years on Mt. Athos in Greece where he was introduced to hesychasm, which is a form of spirituality that places emphasis on interior contemplation rather than external ritualism.

When Sorsky returned to Russia, he established a hermitage, or *skete,* modeled on those on Mt. Athos. Consisting of a simple dwelling for one elder with two disciples, the monks divided their time between prayer, manual labour, study and spiritual counseling for lay people, in exchange for alms. This style of religious life attracted a growing number of monks who were critical of the Church establishment and its brutal treatment of the peasants, who were often tortured with whips and bound in iron shackles.

As hermitages began to spread into remote areas of the Trans Volga region, with a corresponding flight of monks from the monasteries, the Church became increasingly alarmed because it was losing its source of labour. This phenomenon was similar to the Spiritual Franciscans in the West who protested against the power and wealth of the Catholic Church in the 13th and 14th Centuries.

Nil Sorsky and his followers eventually formed a movement, known as the Non-Possessors, a term reflecting their rejection of the material wealth of the Church. To the further annoyance of the Ecclesiastical hierarchy, the Non-Possessors supported a secular heretical movement known as the 'Judaizers', a group that rejected the doctrine of the Trinity as well as advocating the separation of Church and State. The Non-Possessors were critical of the 'Judaizers' in terms of belief. However, they were even more critical of the Church's brutal punishments meted out to the heretics, such as burning at the stake, which in many ways mirrored those of the Papal and Spanish Inquisitions.

The main opponent to Sorsky was Joseph Volokolamsky (1440-1515), founder of the Joseph-Volokokamsk Monastery, which by 1560 was the second largest landowner in Russia. Its vaults also served as a prison for numerous heretics and Non-Possessors, including the renowned scholar Maximus the Greek who spent 14 years in the dungeons of the monastery on the grounds that he supported Sorsky.

Maximus was a highly educated scholar who had studied in Bologna and Florence as well as Mt. Athos where he became a monk. He was invited to Moscow by Vasili III in order to translate works held in the huge library, subsequently referred to as *The Lost Library of the Moscow Tsars,* or the *Golden Library.* It is thought that the library contained valuable Greek, Latin and Egyptian manuscripts, but unfortunately during the reign of Ivan the Terrible, the library was hidden away and has never been found. Not surprisingly, *The Lost Library of the Moscow Tsars* has attracted researchers and archaeologists ever since.

Joseph Volokolamsky and his followers became known as the Possessors, reflecting their views regarding Church property and powers. They are also referred to as the Josephites or Josephinians. Volokolamsky argued that the Church needed the money to maintain schools and hospitals and provide social services and therefore:

'God's holy churches and monasteries must not suffer injury or violence, and their lands and belongings must not be taken away. ...For all Church and monastery property, as well as the fruits of the monks' labour, are dedicated to God. ...He who takes away anything that belongs to a monastery is an offender, and the holy regulations

curse him.' (Article 'House of Hermits', published by Hermitary Resources and reflections on hermits and solitude)

Since both Ivan III and Vasili III were firm supporters of the Josephites, or Possessors, there was no immediate danger of Church property being seized by the State. Nor were the Non-Possessors desirous of acquiring or destroying Church property. Despite the fact that Volokolamsky put up a reasonable argument for the acquisition and maintenance of Church property, his protestations regarding the seizure of property were therefore unfounded.

The Non-Possessors posed a serious challenge for about eighty years, with a few even becoming bishops or metropolitans. Eventually, however, they were no match for the Orthodox Church, which had the backing of the Grand Duke or Tsar. Under the reign of Ivan the Terrible the Non-Possessors were declared heretical and finally destroyed. Yuri's Day, the one day of the year when peasants were permitted to leave their landowning master, was abolished thus binding them to the land for life. This was effectively the beginning of serfdom in Russia.

Although the Non-Possessors as a movement was seriously crushed and their leaders imprisoned, tortured and executed, the ideals that they lived by have never died. Throughout Russian history and to this day, there have been individual lay people, monks and priests who are attracted to the spirituality of hesychasm over against the ritualism of the Russian Orthodox Church.

Ivan IV: The Early Years

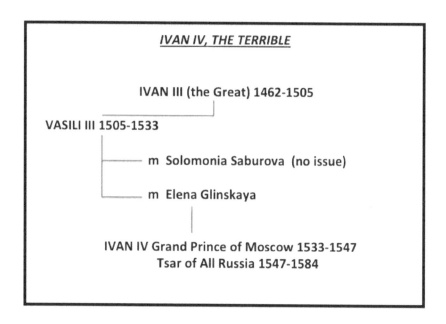

IVAN IV, THE TERRIBLE

IVAN III (the Great) 1462-1505

VASILI III 1505-1533

m Solomonia Saburova (no issue)

m Elena Glinskaya

IVAN IV Grand Prince of Moscow 1533-1547
Tsar of All Russia 1547-1584

Ivan IV, known as the Terrible, was born in August 1530. There has been some debate about his nickname. The word 'terrible' was originally translated from the Russian word *grozny* which at that time meant 'inspiring fear or danger', rather than the more modern connotation of evil or cruel. Ivan was the first son of Vasili III and his mother was Elena Glinskaya, Vasili's second wife. The Tsar had divorced his first wife, Solomonia Saburova, after twenty years of marriage on the grounds that she was barren.

Many in the Church hierarchy disapproved of the divorce, but knowing the necessity for a male heir, Metropolitan Daniel annulled the marriage. Solomonia was sent to a convent. The chronicles say that she went willingly but other sources suggest that she was forced and that she may even have given birth to a child while there. Whatever the truth may be, she ended her life in seclusion and was later canonised by the Russian Orthodox Church as Saint Sofia of Suzdal.

Vasili III died when Ivan was just three years old. While on his deathbed he put the care of his wife Elena and his two sons, Ivan and Yuri, into the hands of Metropolitan Daniel. Elena, Ivan IV's mother, acted as Regent for the next five years during which time she introduced a unified monetary system and strengthened the defensive walls of Moscow. She appeared to have had a compassionate nature that was demonstrated by her paying ransoms for the release of Russian prisoners and introducing measures for the protection of travelers.

Elena, who was chosen by Vasili for her youth and beauty, was the daughter of Prince Vasili Lvovich Glinskaya of the Lipka Tatars, a clan that had settled in Lithuania. Her mother was a Serb Princess. She was not popular among the *boyars*, partly because she had ousted Solomonia, the legitimate wife, but more seriously she was accused of having close political ties with Catholic Lithuania and also a close personal relationship with Metropolitan Daniel. Elena died in 1538 at the age of 27. The cause of death was suspected to be poisoning, a theory that is supported by recent studies of her remains.

The death of the Regent created an opportunity for the *boyars* to reclaim some of the powers they had lost under the centralising policies of Ivan and Vasili. Two competing families in particular rose to prominence: the Shuiskys and the Belskys. For the remaining years of Ivan's minority, the two *boyar* families ruled Muscovy in all but name, while the young boys were totally neglected.

In a letter purported to have been written by Ivan, he said '*My brother Yuri, of blessed memory, and me they brought up like vagrants and children of the poorest. What have I suffered for want of garments and food*'. Even the boys' childhood nurse was banished from the household and anyone else who showed any kindness towards them was severely punished. Publically, however, the *boyars* showed deference towards the boys.

Ivan was an intelligent child and by the age of thirteen he was well aware that he was the legitimate ruler and he decided to reverse the situation. In what was perhaps a first sign of his cruel streak, he ordered the guards to throw one of the Shuisky princes into a cell where he was devoured by hungry dogs.

Ivan, the Tsar of all the Russias

On the 16th January 1547, when Ivan was sixteen, Metropolitan Makarii crowned him with Monomakh's Cap at the Cathedral of the Dormition in Moscow. The Cap was a symbol of Russian autocracy and it first came into use at the time of the Horde. It was in the form of a skullcap, decorated with jewels, trimmed with sable and mounted with a simple gold cross. It is generally thought that the Cap was a gift from Uzbeg Khan and it was used at the coronation of all subsequent Grand Princes and Tsars until the time of Peter the Great who replaced it with a more Western style crown. The original Monomakh's Cap is now kept in the Kremlin Armoury.

Metropolitan Macarii held great influence over the young Ivan. It was he who encouraged the heir to be the first Grand Duke to be crowned with the title 'Tsar of all the Russias'. The title was significant. Whereas Ivan III's use of the title Tsar was purely self-styled, Ivan was officially crowned as such, which put him on a par with earlier Byzantine Emperors. Even more importantly, the coronation by Metropolitan Macarii as 'Tsar of all the Russias', symbolised Ivan's divine right to rule.

Shortly after the coronation, Metropolitan Macarii chose a suitable wife for the new Tsar. She was Anastasia Romanovna Zakarhiina and was the first Russian Tsaritsa. Sixty-six years later, her grandnephew would become the first Romanov Tsar. As was the tradition at the time, Ivan surrounded himself with the families of his new wife as well as the Glinskys, the family of his mother.

On the 24th of June of the same year, a great fire broke out in Moscow, a city built almost entirely of wood. The fire spread into the Kremlin, blowing up the powder stores. Over 3,000 inhabitants lost their lives and about 80,000 lost their homes. The Glinsky family, who had been unpopular with the people ever since Elena arrived from Lithuania to marry Ivan's father, were blamed for the catastrophe and made scapegoats. A rioting crowd, bent on revenge, went in search of the Glinskys who were hiding in the Cathedral of Dormition. One of the Glinsky princes was stoned to death while the rest, including the Tsar's grandmother, fled.

The Glinksy's had played a large part in government affairs and with their downfall Ivan decided to appoint two advisers; Adashef to oversee secular government affairs and Silvester, a priest, with responsibility for spiritual matters. Since Ivan had little interest in affairs of the State, he relied heavily on the two men but when he discovered that they had been plotting with his enemy, the Tatars, he was enraged.

This incident fed into Ivan's growing sense of paranoia. His childhood experiences had taught him to distrust the *boyars*. The violence meted out against his relatives, after the Moscow fire, added to this distrust. The treason of his most trusted advisers further compounded his fear that the *boyars* and princes sought his downfall. His suspicions were not totally unfounded. In April 1564, his most trusted friend, Andrey Kurbsky, defected to Lithuania and joined the Polish-Lithuanian army against Russia. From this moment onwards Ivan vowed that he would do everything in his power to eliminate anyone suspected of treasonable behaviour.

Ivan possessed an uncontrollable anger and had at an early age shown signs of cruelty. During the early years of his reign these traits had been held in check through the influence of both his wife Anastasia and Metropolitan Macarii. By 1560 he had lost both. Macarii had been severely injured during the Moscow fire and in 1560 Anastasia died following a long illness. Ivan immediately suspected the *boyars* of poisoning his wife. Although there was no evidence of this at the time, 20th Century forensic scientists did detect an element of mercury in her remains, but since at that time mercury was used as both a poison and a cure, the discovery proved inconclusive.

Oprichnina 1565-1572

Eight months after the defection of Kurbsky, Ivan travelled with his court and imperial paraphernalia to Alexandrovaskaya Sloboda, near Vladimir. Probably feeling despondent at the time, he threatened to abdicate the throne. When the *boyars* found it difficult to rule in his absence, they appealed for him to return to Moscow. The Tsar agreed to do so, but only on condition that there be no obstruction from either the *boyars* or the Church, to his efforts in rooting out any signs of disloyalty, a condition to which they agreed. Ivan now had a free hand to seek his revenge on the *boyars* and princes.

Ivan's first act was to raise a levy in order to create the *Oprichnina*, meaning 'a place apart'. This was to be a separate territory under the direct rule of the Tsar. He chose the region of Novgorod, which was one of the wealthiest parts of Russia, containing many merchant cities and estates belonging to the *boyars.* Furthermore, Novgorod had, from the time of the Rus', displayed a spirit of independence and had close relations with the Baltic States; both factors that he suspected could lead to dissident tendencies among the people.

A *Boyar* Council ruled the rest of the country, which was called the *zemshchina,* meaning 'land'. Initially Ivan used *zemshchina* institutions in his new territory but he eventually formed independent institutions within the *Oprichnina.* He also set up a personal guard of some 1,000 men, known as the *Oprichniki*, many who came from the *Boyar* class. The *Oprichnik* enjoyed many privileges. The organization increased to some 6,000 and it served as secret police as well as a personal guard. Ivan then began a systematic persecution of the aristocracy.

In situations where a *boyar* owned estates in both the *Oprichnina* and the *zemshchina*, the *Oprichniki* guards seized his lands in the *Oprichnina* and forced the owner, together with his family, servants and peasants into the *zemshchina*. The people made their way on foot, often in mid-winter and anyone who showed them any compassion was immediately executed. It is estimated that out of the 12,000 nobles living in the Suzdal region, 11,000 were sent into exile. Those who remained were often tortured or executed.

Massacre of Novgorod January 1570

Despite Ivan's constant and increasingly violent purges, his sense of paranoia only grew. He became obsessed with the suspicion that his cousin Vladimir of Staritsa was plotting against him. He ordered the *Oprichniks* to burn Vladimir's palace in Moscow and all other lands belonging to him were confiscated. After Ivan accused him of treason, Vladimir and his children were forced to take poison. The prince's wife and mother, who had previously been sent to a convent, were drowned in a nearby river.

A decision to attack Novgorod, which was suspected of planning an alliance with Catholic Lithuania, was taken in the summer of 1569. In January 1570 Ivan's army surrounded the city. The troops spent four days constructing a barrier in order to trap the inhabitants. At the same time, they looted the monasteries and beat the clergy. When the Tsar arrived a few days later, all the clergy, Abbots and monks were beaten to death. Those clergy who escaped death were handed over to the bailiffs, bound in shackles and flogged from dawn to dusk unless they could pay a ransom of 20 rubles.

'Every day he mounted and moved to another monastery, where he indulged his savagery. His men took money, ransacked cells, tore down bells, destroyed equipment and slaughtered cattle. They beat abbots and elders on their heels with sticks...He confiscated treasure in 27 of the oldest monasteries.' (Solov'ev and Rhinelander, *History of Russia*)

Ivan's brutal treatment of the Church was a result of his conviction that the Church hierarchy, and particularly Archbishop Pimen, was planning to transfer allegiance to the Catholic Church.

No one in Novgorod escaped Ivan's terror. Leading merchants were roasted over fires in order to get information regarding traitors. Men, women and children were thrown into the river and trapped under ice. If they managed to surface they were pushed with poles back into the freezing waters.

Apart from the destruction to human life, Ivan ordered the seizure of shops, warehouses and everything of value. The poor were driven out of the city where many died of cold and starvation.

Figures differ as to the actual number of casualties of the massacre, which is said to have lasted five weeks. The *Novgorod Chronicle* and *First Pskov Chronicle,* not surprisingly report a number as high as 60,000. Contemporary Western sources put the number between 3,000 and 27,000 killed.

What is beyond dispute, however, is the devastating effect it had on the city as a whole. Along with his attack on people and property, Ivan's *Oprichniki* burned ninety percent of the arable land resulting in starvation and disease. Novgorod, a city that once over-shadowed and then rivaled Moscow, never did rise to its former glory or economic importance.

In 1572 Ivan decided to disband the *Oprichnina* and reunite the country under the rule of a reformed *Boyar* Council, with members from both the former *Oprichnina* and *zemshchina.* There has been speculation as to why he took this decision. One theory is that Ivan had achieved his aim of destroying the power of the *boyar* class. Another theory is that he had lost confidence in the *Oprichniks* because they failed to offer any effective support during the 1571 Russo-Crimean War.

The Muscovy Company 1555

Despite Ivan's reputation as a cruel despot, not all his actions were destructive. Under his reign the first Russian standing army, the *Streltsy,* was formed and the arts and trade flourished. For example, he established the Moscow Print Yard in 1553, which was to be the first publishing house in Russia. It continued printing books until 1908 when the building became part of the Russian State University for the Humanities.

During his reign, various Eastern khanates pledged allegiance and with the help of the Cossacks, Ivan began the colonisation of the vast regions of Siberia. The Cossacks were ethnic Slavs who lived in remote areas of the rivers Dnieper and Don. They lived in semi-military communities and at that time were totally self-governing.

Ivan showed himself to be an able diplomat, particularly in his relations with England. In 1551, Richard Chancellor and Sir Hugh Willoughby, with the support of Sebastian Cabot, set off from England in three small ships in search of the Northeast Passage to China. All were members of the *Merchant Adventurers to New Lands,* which in 1555 was reformed as the Muscovy Company, becoming the first major chartered joint stock company in England.

Willoughby and two of the ships sailed off course and got stuck in ice near today's Murmansk. Chancellor managed to reach the White Sea. He landed in the harbour of Nikolo-Koreslsky Monastery on the Northern Dvina River, near today's Arkhangelsk. It was a region only recently absorbed into Ivan's empire. When the Tsar heard of Chancellor's arrival, he was immediately invited to Moscow. After a thousand-kilometre trek across snow and ice, Chancellor is reported to have found a city that it was built almost entirely of wood and was much larger than London.

Ivan seized the opportunity of trade with England. He was also keen to develop close relations with a friendly foreign power in order to counter balance his poor relations with Lithuania, Poland and Sweden, all countries that blocked his access to the Atlantic Baltic ports.

He began a correspondence with Queen Elizabeth I and even suggested that an English ship be made available at Arkhangelsk to enable him to escape his enemies, should the need arise.

Chancellor returned to London in 1554 with letters of invitation offering English traders exclusive trading rights and special privileges, such as freedom to set up their own community in Arkhangelsk and immunity from arrest.

This was to be the beginning of a long trading relationship between Russia and England that lasted until the Russian Revolution of 1917. St Andrew's Anglican Church in Moscow was built during Ivan's reign and the Company also supported Anglican churches and ministers in Arkhangelsk.

Today the 'Muscovy Company' is called the 'Russian Company'. It operates within Russia as a charitable organisation with its headquarters in the 'Old English Yard' near the Kremlin and it still supports St Andrews Anglican Church. Sebastion Cabot, a founder of the original company, has monuments and squares around the world named after him, one being Cabot Square in London's Canary Wharf.

Conclusion

Ivan IV has been remembered in history as Ivan the Terrible and it is the 'terrible' side of his life for which he is probably best remembered. But this may do him an injustice when we consider the wider aspects of his long reign of almost fifty years, first as Grand Prince of Moscow and then Tsar of all the Russias.

Ivan's childhood experiences clearly contributed to his unstable and complex personality. Furthermore, despite his acts of terrible cruelty, he was a devoutly religious person. This apparent contradiction was perhaps a consequence of being put into the care of Metropolitan Daniel as a child, followed by the influence of Metropolitan Macarii when he was a young man.

It was Metropolitan Macarii who convinced Ivan that as Tsar of all the Russias, he had a divine right to rule. Consequently, he was convinced that it was a duty to unite his people under the authority of the Russian Orthodox Church and any deviancy would be severely punished, as was the case with the suppression of the Non-Possessors.

His sense of paranoia was two-fold, both of which were with some justification. First, on a personal level it grew out of an almost lifelong fear that the *boyars* wanted to kill him. Second, his relations with Poland-Lithuania were soured by his conviction that its ruler harboured ambitions of spreading Catholicism into Russian territory.

Ivan's reign is also associate d with the creation of the *Oprinchnina,* a 'state within a state' ruled directly by the Tsar. The *Oprinchniki,* his private army, which also acted as a secret police force, could be seen as a forerunner to the 20th Century KGB and today's FSB (Federal Security Service).

While the *Oprinichnina* may have served its purpose in reducing the power of the *boyars,* it resulted in the mass resettlement of people, terrible suffering and economic decline in the region. To Ivan's credit, he disbanded the experiment after seven years.

Under Ivan IV the Grand Principality of Muscovy was transformed into the Tsardom of all Russia. The period witnessed the creation of a standing army, the establishment of a publishing house, law reforms and the beginning of the colonisation of Siberia. It was the beginning of new opportunities for trade, especially with England.

Overall, Ivan's reign could be seen as fairly stable when compared to what was to follow after his death: The Time of Troubles.

*****

CHAPTER SIX

The Time of Troubles

The Time of Troubles refers to the period of social and political upheaval that began with the death of Ivan IV in March 1584 and continued until the accession of Michael I, the first Romanov Tsar of Russia, in 1613.

Ivan the Terrible's first Son, Dmitri, had died in infancy. The Tsar accidentally killed his second son, Ivan, during a violent rage over what he perceived to be his daughter-in-law's inappropriate clothing. This left his third son, Feodor, as successor to the throne.

Ivan had a fourth son, Dmitri, who was born to his seventh wife, Maria Nagaya. Dmitri died in 1591 at the age of eight, just five years after the death of his father.

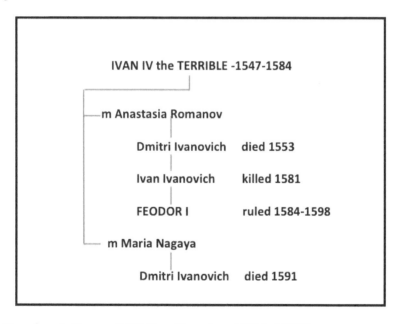

Feodor I: Tsar of All the Russias 1584-1598

Feodor came to the throne at the age of 27. In common with his father, his early life was difficult. He lost his mother Anastasia when he was just three years old, a time when Ivan's excessive cruelty began to manifest itself. He was also said to be frail, both physically and emotionally. He showed little interest in government affairs and found his greatest pleasure in all things religious. He particularly enjoyed church bells and for this reason was known in Russian history as 'Feodor the Bellringer'. His life of devotion also earned him a place in the *Great Synaxaristes* (list of saints and martyrs) of the Orthodox Church, his feast day being the 7th January.

In 1580, Ivan the Terrible arranged for Feodor to marry Irina Godunova who was the sister of Boris Godunov, a senior minister at Ivan's court. It was a successful marriage and Irina became Feodor's greatest support and comforter. A daughter was born several years into the marriage but she only lived for two years. Unfortunately, the couple did not produce a son and consequently the main branch of the Rurik dynasty came to an end with Feodor's death in 1598.

In view of Feodor's frailty, Boris Godunov became *de factor* Regent, while Feodor ruled as nominal Tsar. Despite this, Feodor appears to have shown some interest in government affairs and especially trade and foreign relations. He did not, for example, support his father's policies towards the English. Probably out of an innate sense of fairness, he did not believe that the English should have special privileges and trading rights to the exclusion of other nations, a view that was at odds with Godunova.

The issue resulted in tensions between the Tsar and Godunova and a cooling of relations between England and Russia. Giles Fletcher the Elder, Queen Elizabeth's Ambassador writes:

'The correspondence between the two courts, at the accession of a new sovereign in Russia, was at first tinged with some unpleasantness. The Czar Feodor's first letters to the Queen...contained complaints of the haughty bearing of her envoy, Sir Jerome Bowes...

The Queen, in her answer, dated the 9th of June, 1585...dwells with much emphasis on the constant and peculiar favour shewn by the late Czar Ivan to her subjects, especially in the superior commercial privileges granted to them above all other strangers.' (Giles Fletcher, *Russia at the Close of the Sixteenth Century,* The Hakluyt Society)

Throughout Feodor's reign, the Godunova faction and the Shuisky family jostled for power. The Shuiskys, being a princely branch of the ancient Rurikid dynasty, believed that they represented the legitimate line of succession, whereas the Gudonovs' hold on power was through a tenuous link with Irina Godunova, Tsar Feodor's wife.

The Godunova faction held ambitions of seizing the throne once Feodor was dead. The only real obstacle in their way was Ivan's youngest son, Dmitri, who was the rightful heir to the throne. Probably against the wishes of Feodor, the young prince and his mother Maria Nagaya, together with her brothers, were sent to Uglich on the River Volga. In May 1591, when Dmitri was just eight years old, he died from a stab wound. Some suspected that Godunov was behind the murder. Others believed that the boy somehow survived, escaped and then disappeared. These events led to three 'false Dmitris' or 'pretenders', later claiming the throne.

Leo Tolstoy's acclaimed play, 'Tsar Feodor Ivanovitch', which is part of a trilogy and was performed at the Moscow Art Theatre in 1875, captures the intrigue of the time. The following is an excerpt from a conversation among members of the Shuisky faction:

"Andrei Shouisky (to the clerics) *'Godunoff really reigns - reigns through his sister. By her alone he stands to-day greater and stronger than all the nobles of this land. Already he handles Russia, people and lands and Holy Church, as if it were his own domain. Get rid of his sister - and we can manage him.'*

Vassily Shouisky (reading) *'...We, the clerics, princes, nobles and merchants of all Russia, address you, Majesty! Have mercy upon us, your subjects! Your Tsarina, a Godunoff by birth, has borne you no children, while a great misfortune has befallen your brother, Dmitry Ivanovitch. And should you, through the will of God, be taken from us, your dynasty would become extinct and your kingdom orphaned...Almighty Emperor, be graciously pleased to take another wife unto yourself..."'*

The following shows how the Shuiskys viewed the Tsar:

'"We can get no support from the Tsar. He is like soft putty in the hands of the man who knows how to fashion him. He is not our real ruler. Our real ruler is his brother-in-law, and all Russia clamors for protection against him! Russia looks to us"'.

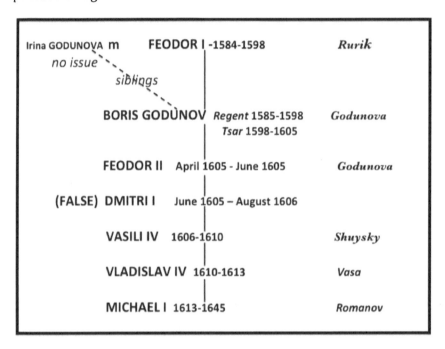

Alexander Pushkin's play *'Boris Godunov'*, written in 1825, tells how Father Pimen, an old monk and chronicler, witnessed the death of the young Dmitri.

"I at that time was sent to distant Uglich upon some mission. I arrived at night. Next morning, at the hour of holy mass, I heard upon a sudden bell toll; 'Twas the alarm bell. Then a cry, an uproar;

Men rushing to the court of the tsaritsa.

Thither I haste, and there had flocked already all Uglich. There I see the young tsarevich lie slaughtered; the queen mother in a swoon bowed over him...

Straightway the people rushed on the three fleeing murderers; they seized the hiding miscreants and led them up to the child's corpse yet warm...

'Confess!' the people thundered; and in terror beneath the axe the villains did confess - and named Boris."

In 1866 Pushkin's play formed the basis of an opera by Modest Mussorgsky, but certain scenes had to be cut out because an imperial decree at the time forbade the portrayal of tsars in opera. This restriction was later limited to just Romanov tsars, which left the way clear for an opera based on the life of Godunov.

Boris Godunov: Tsar of All the Russias 1598-1605

Boris Godunov came from an ancient Tatar clan that in the 14th Century migrated from the Golden Horde to Kostroma, a city located at the confluence of the Volga and Kostroma Rivers. He was at one time a member of Ivan IV's feared *Oprichniki* and moved up in the ranks when he married Maria Skuratova-Belskaya, daughter of the head of the organisation. When Godunov's sister Irina married Tsar Feodor, he was promoted to the rank of *boyar*.

Patriarch Job of Moscow, who was the first Patriarch of Moscow and All Russia, proposed the election of Boris as Tsar on the grounds that as Regent he had proven himself to be an able ruler. The *Zemsky Sobor* (National Assembly) then unanimously endorsed his election and on the 1st September 1598 Godunov was crowned Tsar.

During his reign, Godunov took a great interest in education. He believed that if Russia was to keep pace with intellectual achievements in the West, he needed to attract the best foreign teachers. Apart from recruiting large numbers of Western teachers, he also introduced a programme whereby Russian students were sent overseas for their education. He was also credited with gaining the approval of the Patriarchate of Constantinople for the establishment of an independent Patriarchate of Moscow and All Russia.

Godunov adopted a liberal attitude regarding religion and permitted the Lutherans to build churches in the Empire. This might have been linked to his relations at the time with Sweden, a Lutheran country. In common with many Russian rulers, Godunov's aim was to gain access to the Baltic Sea and his strategy was to form friendly relations, rather than go to war, with the Lutheran Scandinavian countries.

Godunov died of natural causes in April 1605. He left a sixteen-year old son who succeeded him as Feodor II. The boy had received the best of education and had been well prepared for governing. But his rule was to be short-lived. In June of the same year, less than three months after his coronation, agents of the first False Dmitri assassinated him along with his mother.

False Dmitri I: Tsar of All the Russias June 1605- May 1606

When the real Dmitri, the youngest son of Ivan the Terrible, died in 1591, Prince Vasili Ivanovich Shuisky conducted an official inquiry into the death at the request of Godunov. The verdict was that the boy, who apparently suffered from epilepsy, had accidentally stabbed himself while playing with a knife. As mentioned earlier, there was a strong suspicion that Godunov was behind the killing. Another theory was that Dmitri survived the assassination and escaped, while another boy was killed in his place.

In 1600, a young man named Dmitri appeared in Poland claiming to be the son of Ivan IV. His story was that he survived the assassination because his mother, knowing that her son's life was in danger, had placed him in the care of various monasteries. He then fled to Poland where he found employment, possibly as a teacher, with the powerful Wisniowiecki family. Those who had known Ivan the Terrible tended to believe the young man on the grounds of familial resemblance, his aristocratic tendencies, education and fluency in languages.

The Wisniowieckis were Polish magnates of Ruthenian-Lithuanian origin and possibly, even further back, of Rurik descent. They were originally Eastern Orthodox but in common with many among the Orthodox nobility living in the Polish-Lithuanian Commonwealth, had converted to Roman Catholicism and adopted Polish culture. A decision to convert was often motivated by a desire to be seen as a cultured and educated Westerner rather than a backward Easterner. It was this fear of Catholicism encroaching on the Orthodox world that was the root cause of the ongoing tensions between Russia and Poland-Lithuania.

The young man, who became known as False Dmitri I, eventually persuaded sufficient Polish nobles to support his claim to the Russian throne. The Jesuits also agreed to support him on condition that he converted to Catholicism, to which he agreed.

In March 1605, with an army of some 3,500 men, Dmitri marched on Russia. He was joined along the way by many of Godunov's enemies and a large number of Southern Cossacks. Within weeks, however, news spread that Godunov was dead. The way was now almost clear for the False Dmitri to seize the throne.

His first task was to remove the one remaining obstacle: Godunov's son, Feodor II, who had been on the throne for just a few weeks. He imprisoned the new tsar and his mother and then had both strangled. Witnesses claimed that because Feodor was so strong it took four men to hold him down.

False Dmitri then went to his 'father', Ivan IV's grave and he also visited his 'mother', Maria Nagaya, in the monastery where she had been incarcerated since the mysterious death of the real Dmitri. Maria acknowledged False Dmitri as her true son but this was probably for pragmatic reasons since she and all her relatives were subsequently freed and given back their property. When

False Dmitri died a year later, she renounced him as her son, probably realising that it would be in her best interests to do so.

During False Dmitri's short reign, he pardoned many exiles and welcomed their return to Russia. He maintained his close relations with Poland and the Pope and allied with them against the Ottomans. He married Marina Mniszech, a Polish noble woman, assuming that she would convert from Catholicism to Orthodoxy once she was crowned Tsarina. However, this did not happen and it contributed to the general belief that the False Dmitri was too close to Catholic Poland, a situation that that would eventually lead to his downfall.

Prince Vasili Shuisky, head of the *boyars* and former supporter of Godunov, accused the new Tsar of encouraging Lutheranism and sodomy as well as supporting Catholicism. These accusations fueled the anger of the Muscovites who were already upset by the unruly behaviour of the Polish troops who roamed the city and who were allowed to worship in Orthodox churches.

Just ten days after False Dmitri's marriage to Marina, a crowd of *boyars* and Muscovites stormed the Kremlin looking for the Tsar. He managed to escape by jumping out of a window but he was soon captured and executed. His remains were cremated and it is said that the ashes were then shot from a cannon towards the direction of Poland. Most of Dmitri's supporters were massacred but his wife Marina and her father, Jerzy Mniszech, were spared and imprisoned.

False Dmitri II and III

The following year another pretender to the throne appeared on the scene. As with the previous False Dmitri, he was well educated and could speak both Russian and Polish. Jerzy Mniszech seized the opportunity to reunite his daughter Marina with her 'husband'. She surprisingly acknowledged him, even though the Muscovites had executed her real husband the previous year.

In common with False Dmitri I, False Dmitri II received the

support of the Polish nobility and Don Cossacks, as well as large numbers of disaffected Russians. For the next three years his forces were engaged in a civil war against Tsar Vasili IV, the legitimate incumbent of the throne.

In March 1611, a third pretender appeared in Ivangorod, near today's St. Petersburg. Supported by the Cossacks, he was proclaimed Tsar a year later. In May 1612, just two months after his proclamation, he was captured and executed on the orders of Vasili IV.

Vasili IV: Tsar of All the Russias 1606-1610

Following the execution of False Dmitri I, Prince Vasili Shuisky's followers proclaimed him Tsar. He was the only member of the powerful House of Shuisky to ever sit on the throne and he was the last member of the ancient Rurik Dynasty to rule.

As a leading *boyar*, he was unpopular with many Muscovites. He had also proven himself to be untrustworthy and opportunistic. For example, he had supported Godunov over the mysterious death of the real Dmitri. By officially pronouncing the cause of death to be an accident, he diverted the finger of suspicion away from Godunov.

Later, he opportunistically switched sides to support the Polish backed False Dmitri I. Despite the fact that he declared the real Dmitri to have died, he went back on his word and acknowledged the False Dmitri I as the legitimate Tsar.

Vasili survived, however, because there was no better candidate. He was never able to rule effectively and was eventually deposed by a group of *boyars* and forced to become a monk. He was then transported with his brothers to Poland where, in 1612, he died as a prisoner at Gostynin Castle near Warsaw. At the request of the Romanovs, his remains were returned to Moscow in 1635 where they were interred in Archangel Cathedral.

Vladislav IV Vasa: Tsar of All the Russias 1610-1613

The *boyars* who deposed Vasili IV were a group of princes known as The Seven *Boyars*. Among them was Ivan Nikitich Romanov, uncle of Michael Romanov, who was to be the first Tsar of the Romanov dynasty. In the absence of a suitable successor to Vasili IV, as well as the ongoing political instability, the *boyars* decided to invite the Poles to Moscow. This was reminiscent of the early period of Russian history when the Slav tribes of Kievan Rus invited the Varangians to come and rule them. (See Chapter One)

In 1609 the *boyars* invited Prince Vladislav of the Polish house of Vasa, otherwise known as Wladyslaw, to accept the throne. He was just 15 years at the time. However, his father King Sigismund III of Poland and Grand Duke of Lithuania, would only sanction the coronation if Vladislav agreed to impose Catholicism on the people of Russia, thus fulfilling Sigismund's aim of uniting Russia and Poland-Lithuania under Catholicism.

FEODOR II April-June 1605	
Russian	*Polish*
	FALSE DMITRY I 1605-1606
VASILY IV (Shuisky) 1606-1610	
	False Dmitry II
	False Dmitry III
	VLADISLAV IV VASA 1610-1613
MICHAEL ROMANOV 1613-1645	

Vladislav, having a religiously tolerant disposition, refused to do so. His father therefore blocked his accession but agreed that the Prince should rule as Regent. Vladislav made several failed attempts to take Moscow by force but was never able to impose any authority. He simply held a title but had no power. It was a situation that simply added to the ongoing intolerable instability, civil war and misery for the people.

While Vladislav continued to reign as King of Poland and Grand Duke of Lithuania until his death in 1648, Russia was effectively without a ruler since the death of Vasili in 1610. Consequently, the *Zemskiy sobor* decided to elect a new Tsar.

The choice fell on 17 years-old Michael Romanov who was a nephew of Tsar Feodor I, the last of the Rurikid dynasty. The unanimous election of Michael to the as Tsar of All Russia in February 1613 put an end to any further claims to the throng from Vladislav of Poland-Lithuania.

Conclusion

The period between the death of Ivan the Terrible in 1584, and the accession of Michael I in 1613, is aptly named 'The Time of Troubles'. All levels of society were affected, if not by civil war, then by famine.

During the reign of Boris Godunov almost one hundred thousand people died of starvation in Moscow alone. Farmers were not able to produce sufficient food because of constant warfare and anarchy reigned across the land.

There were multiple causes for these troubles. An already weak Russia was caught between two aggressive outside powers: Poland-Lithuania and Sweden. The Poles wanted to absorb Orthodox Russia into its Catholic world, partly in order to help fight the Ottomans. Sweden seized Russian territory in the West in order to create a buffer region to protect her territories along the Baltic coast from the Russians.

The greatest problem, however, was the fact that Russia had no effective ruler. Despite Ivan IV's reputation for cruelty, his reign had been one of relative peace and stability. He had also prepared his son and heir Ivan Ivanovich to succeed him, hoping for a smooth transition of power. But everything went wrong when the Tsar accidentally killed his son during a violent argument. This sparked a constitutional crisis that was to last almost thirty years.

Into the power vacuum that resulted, rival factions fought for the throne. The Shuiskys were *boyars* of the Rurik dynasty and were hated by both the people and the Godunov faction. Vasili Shuisky had also proven himself to be totally untrustworthy. Godunov was equally disliked, both as a perceived imposter and as a suspect for the assassination of the young Prince Dmitri.

The appearance of three pretenders to the throne simply added to the confusion, but more importantly, by backing the False Dmitris, Poland was given an opportunity to intervene in Russia's affairs.

When the *Zemsky Sobor* (Russian Parliament) elected the young Michael Feodorovich Romanov Tsar in February 1613, there came a wind of change. This mild-mannered 17 old was to found a dynasty that would raise Russia to the status of a world power, a power that would survive until its demise in 1917.

*****

CHAPTER SEVEN

Peter the Great

Michael I: Tsar of All the Russias 1613-1645

With the accession of Michael I, the Time of Troubles came to an end. The aim now was to unite and strengthen the country under the new Tsar and rid Russia of foreign occupation. Negotiations began with Sweden aimed at resolving territorial disputes. Sweden wanted the northern port of Arkhangelsk that had previously been acquired under Ivan IV. However, the Dutch and the English held valuable trade concessions through the port and consequently both countries supported Russia against Sweden. A peace treaty was finally signed at Stolbovo, near Lake Ladoga, on 27th January 1617, ending hostilities between the two countries.

In 1618, the Truce of Deulino was signed with the Polish-Lithuanian Commonwealth, ending the 13 years Polish Muscovite War. Under the terms of the Treaty, prisoners were exchanged, including Tsar Michael's father, Feodor Nikitich Romanov, who had been imprisoned with his wife in Poland for eight years.

On returning to Russia, Feodor was made Patriarch of Moscow and all Rus. Known as Patriarch Philaret of Moscow, he became co-ruler with his son Tsar Michael, until his death in 1633.

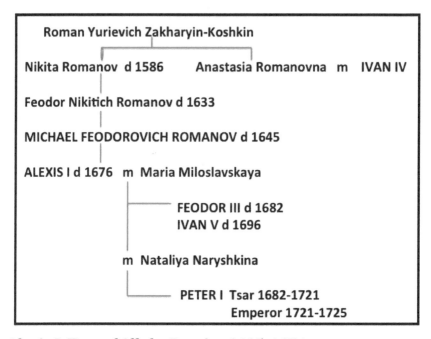

Roman Yurievich Zakharyin-Koshkin

Nikita Romanov d 1586   Anastasia Romanovna   m   IVAN IV

Feodor Nikitich Romanov d 1633

MICHAEL FEODOROVICH ROMANOV d 1645

ALEXIS I d 1676   m Maria Miloslavskaya

FEODOR III d 1682
IVAN V d 1696

m Nataliya Naryshkina

PETER I Tsar 1682-1721
Emperor 1721-1725

Alexis I: Tsar of All the Russias 1645-1676

Alexis I succeeded his father as Tsar in 1645. Since he was only 16 years old, he was put under the tutelage of Boris Morozov, a shrewd and ambitious *boyar*, who led the government for several years. Morozov further secured his position by marrying the sister of Maria Miloslavskaya, who was Alexis' wife.

The first challenge facing Alexis was the Moscow uprising of 1648, also known as the Salt Riot. The trouble began when the government imposed a universal salt tax to cover debts resulting from the Time of Troubles. The taxes fell most heavily on the lower classes, especially the artisans and serfs, while the nobility found ways of tax avoidance. All levels of society felt the impact, however, because a major part of the Russian diet was salt fish that used copious amounts of salt.

Another issue that fueled discontent among the poorer landowners related to escaped serfs. It was commonplace for serfs to run away, either to escape cruel masters, or to find more productive soil. When Alexis came to the throne, landowners were permitted a limited length of time during which they had a legal right to reclaim 'lost souls'. The poorer landowners, who suffered mostly when their serfs escaped, wanted this time restriction lifted, an act that would virtually bind the serfs to their masters for life.

Anger over the salt tax, together with the grievances of landowners, erupted into violence on 1st June 1648. At the time, houses in Moscow were built of wood, and had stoves for heating and cooking. They easily caught fire and around 20,000 of these wooden houses were burned to the ground, with almost 2,000 people losing their lives. The crowds stormed the Kremlin. Boris Morozov escaped with his life, but only on condition that he be sent into exile at the Krillo-Belozersky monastery in Siberia.

In response to the rioting, Alexis promulgated a new legal code, the *Sobornoye Ulozheniye.* A key element of the code, which was to last until 1849, brought slaves and free peasants together under a new 'serf' class which was to be hereditary and permanent. In other words, once born a serf it was impossible to move into another social class. The new legal code also lifted the time restriction regarding escaped serfs, thus formalising bonded serfdom.

During his reign, Alexis also put down a Cossack rebellion in 1671 and negotiated a peace agreement with Safavid Iran following a dispute over territory in the Crimea.

He also expressed his outrage with the English for the beheading of Charles I in 1649. As a result, he broke off diplomatic relations with England. He banned English merchants from the country, including members of the Muscovy Company, while at the same time welcoming Royalist refugees.

Patriarch Nikon and the Old Believers

Religion and the Orthodox Church played a key role in Russian society. From 988, when the Rus' adopted Byzantine Orthodoxy under Vladimir the Great, the Church was to be central to the lives of the people. Grand Dukes, and later Tsars, were no exception. Even Ivan the Terrible would pray for the souls of those he was about to execute in the most gruesome manner.

Tsar Alexis I was particularly religious. His English doctor, Samuel Collins, gives a fascinating insight into the life of Alexis and the Russian people in a letter that he wrote to a friend in 1671. Collins writes that Alexis' lifestyle within the Kremlin was more that of a monk than a Tsar. He would rise at 4am every morning to visit the chapel where he spent many hours in prayer, often accompanied by his wife. He did not drink alcohol and his diet was frugal.

Alexis's spiritual adviser, or confessor, Stefan Vonifatiyev, was a member of a group called Zealots of Piety. The group believed that the suffering experienced during the Time of Troubles was the work of a vengeful God meted out as punishment for the people's sinful ways. Under the leadership of Archmandrite Nikon of the Novospassky Monastery, the group set out their aims: to root out corruption among the clergy, improve the standard of teaching and preaching, to spread the Gospel and fight social injustice.

In order to implement these aims, Nikon, who later became Patriarch of All Russia, believed that a series of reforms were necessary. First he proposed that the divine service books should be revised in order to bring them into line with the Greek Orthodox text, which he considered to be a 'purer' version. His argument was that the books being used by the Russian Church had become tainted by Latin innovations and even printed by Catholics, which was unacceptable.

While the need for reform was generally accepted, many within the Church objected to his proposals regarding a revised text. There were also objections to some of his other proposals, for example, that the sign of the cross should be made by three fingers rather than the traditional two and during the liturgy the 'hallelujah' should be said three times and not two.

Despite these objections and against the will of many clergy and laypeople, Nikon pushed the reforms through. Tsar Alexis supported Nikon and the new prayer books were printed at the Print Yard.

When Nikon was appointed Patriarch in 1652, many of his earlier friends deserted him and a split began to develop between those who supported the reforms and those who objected. The Church hierachy adopted the reforms, which became the official stance of the Russian Orthodox Church. The latter group, those who objected, became known as the Old Believers, or Old Ritualists.

The Great Moscow Synod of 1666, attended by Greek bishops as well as Russian, declared the Old Believers to be heretical and a period of persecution began. Many fled to the forests, to Siberia and other remote regions, where they often became the majority religious group. Some went abroad. Poland-Lithuania, for example, made the refugees welcome and promised them freedom of worship.

Despite centuries of persecution, the Old Believers have survived. When the last imperial census was taken in 1910, approximately 10 percent of the population claimed to be Old Believers. In 1971, the Moscow Patriarchate revoked the anathemas and in 1974 the Russian Orthodox Church Outside Russia did the same, reflecting the fact that large communities of Old Believers now live in many countries of the world.

Feodor III and Ivan V

Feodor III was just 16 years when he succeeded Alexis as Tsar in 1676. He, and his younger brother, Ivan, suffered poor health. Feodor was disabled from birth due to a mysterious illness and Ivan, who was almost blind and feeble, also suffered mental disabilities.

Symeon of Polotsk, an enlightened churchman and academic, was tutor at that time to most of the Tsar's children, including Feodor, Ivan, Sophia and Peter. Symeon had been educated at the Kiev Ecclesiastical Academy and also the Jesuit College of Wilno.

Consequently, he was influenced by Jesuit Catholic theology and was open to Western ideas. Symeon was also present at the Great Moscow Synod in 1666, where he was responsible for drafting the legislation against the Old Believers.

Symeon's ideas were later to influence the young Romanovs. It is most likely that Symeon was an inspiration behind Feodor's policies. During his short reign, for example, the young Tsar founded the Academy of Sciences and ensured that the best professors available were employed to teach Slavonic Greek, Latin and Polish.

Feodor also abolished the *mestnichestvo* system. For generations, government and military appointments had been made according to social status that was meticulously recorded in a 'nobility' book. Feodor ordered all such books to be destroyed and that henceforth appointments were to be decided on merit.

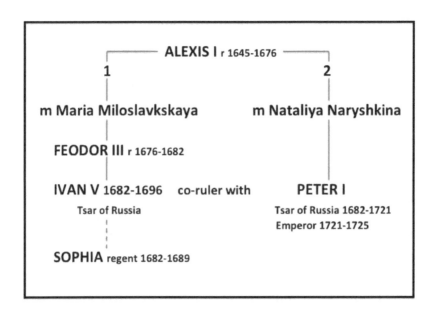

Sophia Alekseyevna

When Tsar Alexis married Nataliya Naryshkina after the death of his first wife Maria Miloslavskaya, rivalry erupted between the families of the two wives. Sophia Alekseyevna, the third surviving daughter of Tsar Alexis with Maria Miloslavskaya, openly championed the succession of Ivan against the young Peter, son of Nataliya Naryshkina.

From an early age, Sophia had shown a determination and strength of will almost unheard of among women of Russian nobility of the time. She persuaded her father Alexis to allow her to join her brothers Feodor, Ivan and Peter in their studies with Symeon of Polotsk. Consequently she was their equal in terms of education.

At that time women of the court were traditionally hidden away in the *terem*, (the upper part of the palace or castle). They were not permitted to socialise with men beyond their immediate family. If they did leave the *terem* they were fully veiled and hidden behind heavy curtains when travelling in carriages, a practice influenced by the Byzantines. Furthermore, all women were subjugated under the strict code of the *Domostroy,* meaning 'social order', to a status little above servants, or in some cases, slaves. The code was put in place during the reign of Ivan the Terrible in the 16th Century as guide to running a good household. Most of the *Domostroy* is now obsolete although some elements are still popular today with traditionalists.

For example, regarding marriage, a couple was expected to love God before each other. On the place of women:

'In all affairs of everyday life, the wife is to take counsel with her husband, and to ask him, if she needs anything...

If a woman was unchaste, then:

'Husbands should not use wooden or iron rods on their wives, or beat them round the face, ears or abdomen, lest they cause blindness, deafness, paralysis, toothache or miscarriage.'

Moscow Uprising of 1682

Feodor III died in 1682 after a reign of just six years. Next in line for the throne was the fifteen years old Ivan who, although intelligent and well educated, was not fit to rule because of his disabilities. Peter was therefore chosen as successor.

At this point, Sophia openly declared her opposition to the choice of Peter on the grounds that Ivan was the legitimate heir since he was the son of Alexis' first wife. Then rumours began to circulate among the *Streltsy* (troops) that the Naryshkina family had murdered Ivan. While it is possible that Sophia instigated these rumours, there is little doubt that she, and her Miloslavky supporters, stirred up the riots that followed.

On the 11th May 1682, an angry mob of *Streltsy*, joined by disaffected Moscovites including Old Believers, marched on the Kremlin. The terrified Nataliya grabbed the young boys Ivan and Peter and faced the crowds, as proof that the Ivan had not been harmed. Temporarily calm was restored, but the crowds still sought revenge against the *boyars* for their many grievances. A second attack was made, resulting in the brutal murder of scores of *boyars* and members of the Naryshkina family. Peter watched in horror as his uncles were thrown from the steps of the Kremlin onto spikes on the ground below. The boy was motionless, but the brutality that he witnessed on that day was to affect him for life. Crucially, he developed a hatred of the *Streltsy* and a loathing for Moscow.

Eventually it was decided that Ivan should co-rule as Tsar with his younger half-brother Peter. A special two-seater throne was commissioned for the coronation that took place on the 26th June 1682 at the Cathedral of Dormition in Moscow.

Since neither the weak Ivan, nor the ten years old Peter, were able to rule, the Regency was put into the hands of their elder sister, Sophia Alekseyevna. During her seven years as Regent, Vasily Golitsyn acted as her chief adviser. He had previously served at the courts of Alexis and Feodor III and was an able statesman who was open to reform. In foreign affairs, he was instrumental in agreeing the Chinese-Russian border and formulating a peace treaty with Poland. His unsuccessful Crimean campaigns, however, resulted in him losing his popularity with the people.

When Peter came of age he gradually replaced the Miloslavkys with his Naryshkina relatives. Sophia tried once again to rouse the *Streltsy* against the Naryshkinas, but she failed to get their support and consequently Peter confined her to a convent. At this point she was not made to take the veil, but ten years later, following an even more serious *Streltsy* uprising, Peter forced her into a life of total seclusion. She died at the age of 46 in the Novodevichy Convent in Moscow.

Peter's Early Reign

When Ivan V died in 1696, Peter became sole ruler. He was 24 years old, well over six feet tall with disproportionately long arms. It is also said that he had a small head for his height and dark eyes, probably inherited through his mother's Tatar ancestry. When under stress he developed a slight facial twitch, possibly as a result of his traumatic childhood experiences.

From a very early age Peter was interested in all things military, initially playing with toy soldiers but later he and his friends formed their own units to play mock war games. They also had small boats that they took out on a lake to engage in mock naval battles.

When Peter came to the throne his priority was to reform the army and build a navy. He viewed the *Streltsy*, with their long, ragged beards and cumbersome red coats, as a medieval, ill-disciplined rabble that needed replacing with a disciplined army modeled on Western lines. In order to achieve this, he invited military experts from Western Europe to Russia to help with the task. Apart from adopting Western style uniforms, Peter's armies were required to wear moustaches and have their hair cut above the shoulders.

Attempts to reform the *Streltsy* proved unpopular with both the troops and the people but Peter asserted his authority and quickly put down any sign of rebellion.

Another major reform, that affected the wider population, concerned dress. He forced the court, and encouraged the people, to give up their traditional Russian style clothing, and adopt Western dress. In an attempt to improve the manners of the people, he commissioned the 'The Honest Mirror of Youth', which was a manual on etiquette covering such things as how to spit, or clear the nose.

Peter's greatest target was the beard that symbolised for him much that was wrong with Russia. In particular, the beard was symbolic of the backwardness of the *Streltsy* and the Church.

Unlike most of Peter's predecessors, he was not particularly religious. He believed, as did other Western monarchs at the time of the Enlightenment, that the conservatism of the institutional Church held back the transition of Russia into a modern nation.

In 1698, two years after he assumed sole power, Peter introduced a tax on those who insisted upon wearing traditional dress or sporting a beard. For the religiously conservative Old Believers, the idea of shaving off their beards was seen as incompatible with their beliefs. Consequently, they became a target of the state police. Peter himself never grew a beard and in portraits he is generally shown wearing military dress.

In 1700 Peter introduced legislation that affected the Church. When the Patriarchate became vacant he refused to allow the Church to appoint a replacement. Instead he set up a Holy Synod that was accountable to a secular bureaucrat, while he assumed personal responsibility for appointing bishops. He also believed that too many young men were entering monasteries where their skills and talents were wasted. Since he preferred to have them enlist in his reformed army and later his navy, he ruled that no man should enter a monastery before the age of 50.

The Grand Embassy

In 1697 Peter led a diplomatic mission, totaling some 250 members, to Europe. Ostensibly the purpose was to seek support from Western nations, and particularly the Holy Roman Empire, for his war against the Ottomans in the Crimea. His other agenda was to learn as much as he could about shipbuilding and Western expertise in general.

For much of the time he travelled incognito in order that he could get some hands-on experience and also avoid the tedious and time-consuming formalities of a State visit. All members of the delegation were ordered to secrecy about his identity, but since he was unusually tall for the time, he was very often recognised and word soon spread that he was present within the group.

While in the Netherlands he spent almost four months working in the shipyard of the Dutch East India company, which at the time was one of the largest in the world. He also engaged many shipwrights and seamen who would later help with his new navy.

Peter then went on to England where he met King William III. He also visited Greenwich and the Royal Naval dockyard at Deptford. He learned about city planning when he visited Manchester and this was to influence his ideas when building his own city of St. Petersburg. He then visited Vienna to meet with the Elector of Saxony, Augustus II the Strong and Leopold I, the Holy Roman Emperor. In June, 1698 his trip had to be curtailed. Once more the *Streltsy* had rebelled.

Streltsy Rebellion of 1698

While Peter was away in Europe, discontent spread through the *Streltsy* regiments. This was partly due to opposition to the Tsar's reforms, but also general anger over their poor conditions and lack of food. Some of their leaders secretly made contact with Peter's sister and ex Regent, Sophia Alekseyevna, who had been sent to Novodevichy convent ten years earlier. The *Streltsy* were hoping that Sophia would mediate with the Tsar on their behalf.

On 6th June, some 2,500 *Streltsy* marched on Moscow from Azov where they had been stationed. Peter ordered four of his regiments, under the command of Patrick Gordon, a Scottish soldier of fortune, to put down the rebellion. Gordon's men defeated the *Streltsy* on the 18th June near the New Jerusalem

Monastery, just West of Moscow.

The Tsar was merciless in his revenge. He employed the most brutal forms of torture including whipping victims to death and roasting them over fires. Some 1,200 men were executed and many hundreds were sent into exile in Siberia.

Those *Streltsy* regiments that had not taken part were simply disbanded. It was the end of the *Streltsy.*

It was also the end of Sophia. Although she escaped with her life, she might well have been dead, because now Peter insisted that she lose all her previous privileges. She was to be confined to a small cell in strict seclusion and on a simple diet. It is said that to add to her misery, Peter arranged for the corpses of dead *Streltsy* to hang outside her window: a view from which she could not escape. She survived for another six years.

The *Streltsy* rebellion, like many other major events in Russian history, was the subject of an opera. Mussorgsky's unfinished opera, *The Khovansky Affair,* was set against the conflict between the reformers and traditionalists and conflates the Moscow Uprising of 1682 with the 1698 Rebellion.

St. Petersburg

If Peter's ambitions for a great navy were to be achieved, then he obviously needed access to the sea. Since the northern port of Arkhangelsk was icebound for many months of the year, he desperately needed a warm water port. In the East, while his troops had taken the fortress of Azov in 1696, he had never succeeded in gaining further territory from the Ottomans that would have given him access to the Black Sea.

His other option was to gain access to the Baltic Coast in the West, by acquiring Swedish territory. For 21 years, between 1700 and 1721, war raged between Sweden and an alliance made up at various times of Denmark-Norway, Saxony and Poland-Lithuania and Russia. The conflict is known as the Great Northern War, during which time Sweden was forced to defend its territory.

Under the terms of the peace treaty that ended hostilities, Russia acquired Livonia, Latvia and Estonia.

In May 1703, during the War, Russia seized the Nyenskans fortress at the mouth of the River Neva. A few days later Peter laid the foundations, on Zayachy Island, of the Peter and Paul Fortress. These were to be the first bricks of what became St. Petersburg.

Alexander Danilovich Menshikov, a Russian statesman who had accompanied Peter on his European tour, was given overall responsibility for building the city. Peter chose a Frenchman, Jean-Baptiste Alexandre Le Blond as the chief architect. His choice might have been influenced by the magnificence of Versailles and a desire to produce a city of similar grandeur.

Conscripted peasants, serfs and Swedish prisoners laboured to build the city. They had few tools. The ground was boggy and they were forced to carry soil in their shirts. Poor conditions and an unrelenting regime resulted in tens of thousands of deaths.

In 1712, while the region was still officially part of Sweden, Peter moved the capital city from Moscow to St. Petersburg. Apart from a short period under the rule of Peter II, St. Petersburg remained the capital of Russia until 1918. In modern times the name of the city has changed several times reflecting the politics of the day. In 1914 it was named Petrograd, in 1918, Leningrad and in 1991 after the fall of Soviet Union it reverted to St. Petersburg.

Marriages and Mistresses

In 1689, when Peter was about 17 years, his mother arranged for him to marry Eudoxia Lopukhina a daughter of minor nobility. She was to be the last Russian born Tsarina. She bore him three sons but only one survived, Alexei Petrovich, who became heir to the throne.

It was not a happy marriage, largely because Peter found Eudoxia and her relatives far too conservative. In 1671, on one of his frequent visits to the German quarter of Moscow, he met Anna Mons, daughter of a Dutch wine merchant. She became his official mistress and the relationship lasted for about 12 years.

When Peter returned from his European tour in 1698, he divorced Eudoxia and she was forced to enter a convent. At the same time he declared that arranged marriages should be discouraged because the couple may not like each other, which could lead to violence.

Anna Mons had hopes that Peter would marry her once he was divorced, but she was to be disappointed. Instead he took another mistress, Marta Samuilovna Skavronskaya who was later to become Empress Catherine I of Russia.

There are various accounts of Marta's early life, but it is generally thought that her father was a Roman Catholic peasant from Poland-Lithuania and her mother was German. When both parents died of the plague it is said that she was taken in by a Lutheran pastor as a servant. She worked as a servant in various households gradually moving up the social ladder until she found herself in the service of Alexander Danilovich Menshikov, the close friend of Peter the Great who had been put in charge of building St. Petersburg.

Peter met Marta in 1703 while visiting Menshikov's house and by 1704 she had become the Tsar's official mistress. She gave birth to a son, Peter, changed her name to Catherine and converted to Orthodoxy.

On the 9th February 1712, the couple married at St Isaac's Cathedral in St. Petersburg. In commemoration of the marriage, Peter instituted The Imperial Order of St. Catherine. Today, Maria Vladimirovna, Grand Duchess of Russia and the Great-Great-Granddaughter of Tsar Alexander II of Russia, claims the title of Grand Mistress of the Order.

Peter and Catherine eventually had twelve children but only Anna and Elizabeth survived. In 1721, when Peter raised Russia to the status of Empire, Catherine became Empress Consort.

Throughout Eudoxia's incarceration in a convent, many nobles and churchmen, who were opposed to Peter's reforms, supported her. Peter suspected that his son by Euroxia, Alexei, was plotting with them to overthrow him. In June 1718 Alexei was arrested, tried and condemned to death for treason. But before the execution could take place Alexei had died from excessive torture.

Conclusion

Peter the Great is often credited with transforming Russia from a backward, medieval Asiatic country into a modern Westward looking nation that could stand alongside European states. It is true that during Peter's reign there were many reforms but the transition really began under his predecessors.

Peter's father, Alexis, had been more interested in the spiritual life than government affairs and he elder brother Feodor was extremely frail. It is highly unlikely therefore that they would have been behind the various reforms took place at the time.

It is most likely that either Symeon of Polotsk, tutor to Alexis' children, or Vasily Golitsyn, adviser to Sophia Alekseyevna were behind the founding of the Academy of Sciences which employed the best professors in Slavonic Greek, Latin and Polish. The same could be said regarding the abolition of the *mestnichestvo* system, which made appointments according to social status rather than on merit.

Both Symon and Golitsyn were able men who were open to Western ideas. Both men were influential at the courts of Alexis, Feodor and Peter.

Peter seems to have been particularly affected by the experience of witnessing his uncles being brutally murdered when he was a young child. It was an experience that resulted in a lifelong hatred of the *Streltsy*. He also seems to have developed, as so many of his predecessors, an obsession that others were plotting against him.

Unlike many previous rulers, Peter did not appear to be particularly religious. Furthermore, he appeared to have little regard for Church authority, an example being when he refused to allow the Church to appoint a new Patriarch. Although he welcomed the reforms proposed by Patriarch Nikon, he believed that Nikon, with his overweening power posed a threat to his authority.

With the help of Western expertise, he modernised the army and created a navy. He provided Russia with an outlet into the Baltic Sea and founded the modern city of St. Petersburg, but at the cost of many lives. He introduced Western ideas, fashion and etiquette

Despite his progressive, Western ideas, he could be as brutal, indeed barbaric, as his predecessors. He could even be accused of being even more cruel than Ivan the Terrible when it came to the death of his own son. Ivan had killed his son accidentally in a fit of rage: Peter killed his son in cold blood following days of torture.

*****

CHAPTER EIGHT

Coups and Conspiracies

Peter the Great died on the 8th February 1725 following a bladder infection that had worsened with the onset of gangrene. He was 53 years old. His death ushered in a period of instability analogous to the Time of Troubles following the death of Ivan the Terrible.

For almost fifty years, opposing court factions, backed by the Palace Guard, plotted and schemed to get their favoured candidate on the throne. Parties divided along various lines. There were those who wanted the succession to follow in a direct line from Peter I, and those who believed that descendants of his brother and co-heir Ivan, were equally eligible. Also, depending on which Tsar was on the throne, foreign policy changed from being either anti-Prussia or pro-Prussia.

There was also a split between the traditional Muscovites who favoured Moscow as the Imperial capital, and the reformers who preferred the new city of St. Petersburg. The reformers included Alexander Menshikov and Peter Tolstoy, ancestor of the novelist Leo Tolstoy. The conservatives included Dmitri Golitzyn, who had never forgiven Peter I for divorcing his first wife Eudoxia.

As a result of this instability, three Empresses and three Emperors were to rule Russia in the short period between 1725 and the accession of Catherine the Great in 1762.

Catherine I, Empress of All the Russias 1725-1727

The first to rule was Peter's foreign-born wife Catherine, who succeeded him as Catherine I, Empress and Autocrat of all Russia. (Not to be confused with Catherine the Great)

As mentioned in the previous Chapter, Catherine's early life is shrouded in mystery. She was born Marta Helena Skowroriska in 1684 in Semigallia, today's Latvia, which was then part of the Polish-Lithuanian Commonwealth. Her mother was German and her father is variously reported as being a Polish peasant, a

Swedish soldier, a gravedigger or a runaway serf.

By the age of nineteen Catherine, at the time known as Marta, was in the service of Prince Alexander Menshikov, the close friend of Peter the Great. It is possible that she became Menshikov's mistress. What is certain, however, is that Menshikov and Catherine had an extremely close relationship that survived until Catherine died in 1727.

Menshikov rose to power during the reign of Peter I. He held many titles, including Generalissimus, Prince of the Russian Empire, Duke of Ingria and Prince of the Holy Roman Empire. He had travelled to Holland and England with Peter and worked alongside the Tsar in the shipbuilding yards. Above all, Menshikov shared Peter's passion for reform.

When Peter died in 1725, Menshikov's main concern was that the programme of reform should continue. With this in mind, he instigated the accession of Catherine to the throne believing that she would support his proposal that while she ruled in name, he would be the real power behind the throne. Bearing in mind that Catherine had once been a servant in his household, and possibly his mistress, the plan was likely to succeed.

Menshikov also persuaded Catherine to set up a Supreme Privy Council, with himself at its head, to act as her advisory body. Catherine proved to be a popular choice among the nobles, since coming from humble origins, she would be unencumbered by a retinue of relatives seeking favoured positions at court.

Catherine's reign only lasted two years and during this time Menshikov effectively ruled the Empire. On one issue, however, Catherine took the lead. She had inherited a vast army of over 200,000 men. Being possibly the largest European army at the time, it used up around sixty percent of the imperial budget. By reducing military costs Catherine was able to reduce taxation, a policy that proved to be popular with the people.

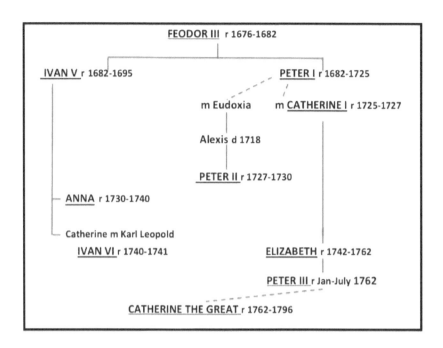

FEODOR III r 1676-1682

IVAN V r 1682-1695   PETER I r 1682-1725

m Eudoxia   m CATHERINE I r 1725-1727

Alexis d 1718

PETER II r 1727-1730

ANNA r 1730-1740

Catherine m Karl Leopold

IVAN VI r 1740-1741   ELIZABETH r 1742-1762

PETER III r Jan-July 1762

CATHERINE THE GREAT r 1762-1796

Peter II, Emperor of All the Russias 1727-1730

Under the influence of Menshikov, the Supreme Privy Council chose 12 years old Peter, the grandson of Peter the Great, to succeed Catherine. In order to strengthen his position, Menshikov then arranged the betrothal of his daughter, Maria, to the new Tsar.

Although Peter II, being in the direct line of succession, was the rightful heir, he was ill prepared for the task. Peter the Great had never liked the young Peter. This probably stemmed from his dislike of his first wife Eudoxia, who was the boy's grandmother. This dislike was then transferred to Alexis, his son by Eudoxia. It is likely that the young Peter reminded the Tsar of Alexis, the son he had tortured and executed.

Consequently, from the time Peter II was orphaned at the age of three, he and his sister were virtually ignored and little attention was paid to their education. Once Peter I had died, Menshikov stepped in and arranged for Peter II to be tutored by Count

Ostermann, a German born statesman who had served under Peter the Great.

Following Peter II's coronation, Menshikov assumed complete control of the young Emperor by taking him into his home where he could watch every move. Eventually the young Tsar rebelled against Menshikov's bullying and with the support of Ostermann, Menshikov was deposed and exiled with his family to Siberia.

During his reign, Peter II moved the court from St. Petersburg back to Moscow, the city where his grandmother Euroxia had felt most at home. His reign was to be short lived however. He died from smallpox in January 1730 at the age of 14 years. His death marked the end of the direct male line of the Romanov Dynasty.

Anna, Empress of All the Russias 1730-1740

Anna was the daughter of Ivan V, who co-ruled with Peter I from 1682 until his death in 1695. She was one of five daughters, three of whom survived to adulthood. Anna's mother, Praskovia Saltykovia, remained a widow following Ivan's death and she dedicated her life to the strict upbringing of her daughters.

Anna received a rounded education that included languages, religion and music. But from an early age she showed a lack of compassion, even finding delight in others' suffering. It was a trait that would increase during her lifetime to the point where she became so cruel that she earned the nickname 'Iv-anna The Terrible'.

One particular incident illustrates her warped sense of humour and cruel streak. In celebration of Russia's victory over the Ottomans in 1739, she arranged a special festival. The winter that year was particularly cold and she ordered the construction of an ice palace complete with an ice garden with ice birds and statues. The palace also contained ice furniture including an ice bed.

Anna then forced a senior member of the Golitsyn family to go through a mock marriage with one of her least attractive maids. The couple was then made to spend the night, naked, on the ice bed of the ice palace. They only survived the ordeal because a guard agreed to exchange his sheepskin coat for the bride's necklace.

Peter Yeropkin, who designed much of St. Petersburg, was the architect of the ice palace. He left a record of his work and an ice palace has been recreated in St. Petersburg every year since then.

When Anna was 17 years old, her uncle Peter the Great arranged for her to marry the Duke of Courland, but shortly after the marriage the Duke died. Anna chose not to marry again but she went on to rule her husband's Dukedom until 1730, when she became Empress of Russia.

Anna was not the obvious choice to succeed to the throne. She had an older sister and there were Peter's two surviving daughters, both of whom might have had a stronger claim had they been older and had they not been born out of wedlock. (They were born to Catherine before she married Peter I) Anna also had two further advantages. First, she was a widow and childless. Second, her almost twenty years governing her late husband's province of Courland was proof of her ability to rule.

However, the Supreme Privy Council was keen to restrict her power by laying down certain 'conditions' to her rule. Dmitry Golitsyn was the inspiration behind the 'Conditions', which read:

We hereby give a most binding promise that my main concern and effort shall be not only to maintain but to spread, as far as possible and in every way, our Orthodox faith of the Greek Confession. Moreover, after accepting the Russian crown, I will not enter into wedlock so long as I live; nor will I designate a successor, either in my lifetime or after. We also promise that, since the safety and welfare of every state depends upon good counsel, we will always maintain the Supreme Privy Council as it is at present established with its membership of eight persons. Without the consent of this Supreme Privy Council:

We will not start a war with anybody

We will not conclude peace...

We will not spend any revenues of state

...Should I not carry out or fail to live up to any part of this promise, I shall be deprived of the Russian crown. (Documents in Russian History)

In January 1730 Anna signed the document, which was clearly intended to restrict her powers in favour of the Supreme Privy Council. Historians have suggested that this was an early attempt to introduce constitutional a monarchy in Russia.

Two months later another faction, including Anna's elder sister, protested that the 'Conditions' placed too much power into the hands of the Supreme Privy Council. They persuaded her to disband the Council and tear up the 'Conditions'. This she did and the leading members of the Council and architects of the 'Conditions' were either executed or sent to Siberia. Golitsyn survived the purge. The Empire returned to its traditional form of autocracy and Anna assumed supreme power as Empress and Autocrat of All Russia.

Anna ruled for ten years and in common with other women empresses and queens in history, and particularly Russian history, it was rumoured that she had a lover who wielded the real power behind the throne. In Anna's case it was Ernst Johann von Biron who was Duke of Courland and Semigallia, the province that she had ruled following her husband's death.

Biron surrounded himself with German advisers and this period has been described as the *Bironovshchina*, meaning the 'German Yoke'. He made many enemies among the Russian nobility and he was ruthless in putting down dissent. Apart from hundreds of executions, he also sent many thousands to exile in Siberia.

Anna and Biron continued Peter's policies for reforming the Russian Orthodox Church. Peter had abolished the patriarchate replacing it with the Holy Governing Synod that included lay members as well as clerics. The implementation of Peter's reforms, often forcefully, led to widespread persecution of the clergy.

At the time of Anna's reign, the head of the Holy Governing Synod was Feofan Prokopovich. He was a Ukrainian Russian of humble origins. Possessing a brilliant mind, he rose to become Archbishop of Novgorod before assuming responsibility for the Holy Governing Synod. As a young man, Prokopovich had spent time studying in Rome and for a short while he professed the Catholic Faith. After leaving Rome, he passed through Switzerland and Germany where he became influenced by Protestantism, and particularly Lutheranism.

Throughout his career he had shown disdain for the conservative elements of the Russian Orthodox Church and this was exacerbated by his positive experience with the Roman Catholic Church and even more so by the influence of Lutheranism. In his determinism to root out any resistance to reform, he ordered hundreds of priests and bishops to be tortured and imprisoned. This continued throughout Anna's reign. When those who survived were finally released, they were so severely damaged that none were strong enough to resume clerical duties.

Despite Anna's eccentricities, the unpopularity of Biron's German party and persecutions in the Church, there were some positive developments during her reign.

She continued where Peter left off in building St. Petersburg and she founded a Cadet Corps for the military training of young boys. One of her most successful enterprises was her continued funding and support for the Russian Academy of Science that was founded by Peter the Great. Although only small in student numbers, the Academy commissioned Western tutors and one of its most significant projects at that time was its exploration of the Bering Sea.

Anna was a great supporter of the arts and during her reign the curriculum of the Academy was widened to include the theatre, architecture and literature. The foundation of the Russian Ballet also occurred at the same time.

In terms of foreign policy, the greatest emphasis was on the East; first securing territory around the city of Azov against opposition from the Ottomans and second, agreeing peace terms with the Persians on land in the Caucasus. Anna also received embassies from China, which is an indication of the importance that China placed on the rising power of Russia.

Anna died from kidney stones in October 1740 at the age of 47. Just before her death she pronounced her successor to be her grandnephew Ivan VI who was then only two months old. Her intention was that Biron should act as Regent. By choosing Ivan, she was securing the succession down the line of Ivan V, rather than Peter the Great and by nominating Biron, she was ensuring that her lover held on to power.

Ivan VI: nominal Emperor of All the Russias October 1740-December 1741

Anna's plans were to be thwarted. The appointment of Biron as Regent angered not only the child Emperor's parents, but also the nobility among whom he had many enemies. Just three weeks after Anna's death, Biron was arrested and condemned to death by quartering. However, with the intervention of Anna Leopoldovna, the child's mother, the sentence was commuted to exile in Siberia. With Biron in exile, Anna Leopoldovna became Regent for her baby son while Osterman effectively ran the government.

Throughout the latter years of Empress Anna's reign and the Regency of Anna Leopoldovna, Elizabeth, Peter the Great's daughter with Catherine, was scheming ways to gain the throne for herself. As the daughter of Peter I, many viewed her as the legitimate heir. Others wanted to oust the growing number of Germans who had surrounded Empress Anna. Consequently, Elizabeth had many supporters among the nobility and she was also extremely popular with the Palace Guard.

On the 24th November 1741, at the instigation of Elizabeth, the

Preobrazhensky Regiment of the Palace Guards marched on the Winter Palace and seized the young Emperor along with his mother. On the 6th December 1741, Elizabeth succeeded to the throne as Empress of All Russia.

Initially Ivan VI and his family were imprisoned together, but in 1744 Elizabeth sent the child to a remote region of the White Sea. He was to spend the rest of his life imprisoned and in isolation. His name was subject to *Damnatio memoriae* with the intention that his name should never be mentioned and his existence erased from memory. This was to avoid any possible challenge to Elizabeth.

In July 1764, during the subsequent reign of Catherine the Great, Vasily Mirovich, one of Ivan's jailors discovered his identity. All the jailors were under strict instructions to kill the boy should anyone try to release him. When Mirovich suggested releasing the prisoner, Ivan was immediately killed. He was 23 years old.

Empress Elizabeth of All the Russias: 1741-1762

Elizabeth was Peter the Great's second daughter to survive to adulthood with his second wife Catherine. It is said that she resembled her father both physically and in temperament but even though she was her father's favourite child, she only received a basic education. This might have been because she would not have been considered an obvious candidate for the throne. Peter had a son and grandson from his first wife Eudoxia, both of whom could have a greater claim. Furthermore, Elizabeth's legitimacy was questionable because she was born out of wedlock.

Despite the fact that her education had been neglected, Elizabeth had a flair for languages and, like her father, enjoyed physical activities such as hunting, riding and gardening. She was described as having light brown hair, blue eyes, good teeth and a nice mouth.

Elizabeth was a great sponsor of the arts and had her own choir. Once she became Empress she reveled in lavish balls, her favourites being the masked ball and the Metamorphoses ball whereby guests were required to dress as the opposite sex. Many ladies of the court disliked these Metamorphoses balls but Elizabeth, who was tall and well built, thoroughly enjoyed them and she looked good dressed in military uniform or as a Cossack.

Although full of fun and said to be warm-hearted, she was extremely vain. She reputedly never wore the same dress twice and forbade the ladies of the court to wear any dress or accessory similar to her own. She also ensured that no expense was spared in terms of food, drink, decor and music, making her court equally, if not more lavish than any in Europe. Foreign diplomats often commented that while the Russian nobility wore the finest and most expensive clothes and jewelry, they might ride in a broken down old carriage to a dilapidated home.

Another aspect of Elizabeth's character that is worth mentioning is that on ascending the throne she declared that she would never pass a death sentence. Apart from ordering the killing of Ivan VI, who was a threat to her position, she kept to her word throughout her reign. She did not, however, restrict the use of brutal torture.

Elizabeth's father Peter had hopes of marrying his children off to European royalty, so consolidating Russia's position in Europe. While he was able to marry his son Alexei into the German house of Brunswick-Luneburg, he had less success with his daughters. All his overtures to the great European dynasties were rejected on the grounds that the girls' mother had started life as a servant girl and furthermore, they were born out of wedlock.

Eventually Peter managed to secure the betrothal of both girls to two princes of the minor German house of Holstein-Gottorp. Unfortunately, Elizabeth's betrothed, Charles August of Holstein-Gottorp, died just before the wedding. By the age of 17 years she had lost not only her fiancé, but also both parents. Without a patron, her chances of securing a good marriage were extremely remote.

Being a beautiful and outgoing young woman and with no

prospect of marriage, Elizabeth not surprisingly took a handsome young officer of the Palace Guard as her lover. When Empress Anna, nicknamed 'Iv-anna the Terrible', discovered the affair, she had the unfortunate man's tongue cut out before banishing him to Siberia.

Elizabeth was later to take Ukrainian born Cossack, Alexei Razumovsky, as her long-term lover. Apart from being handsome, Razumovsky had a fine voice and he was invited to join the choir in the Palace chapel. Once Elizabeth became Empress, Razumovsky received numerous honours as well as landed estates. It was also rumoured that the couple had secretly married. The possibility that they might have had children has been the subject of various plays and films. The 1930s French film entitled *Tarakanova*, for example, tells the story of a woman who claimed to be the daughter of Elizabeth and Razumovsky.

Elizabeth wisely appointed Alexey Bestuzhev-Ryumin as her minister for foreign affairs. Bestuzhev's father was a Russian Ambassador and he and his brother had been educated in Copenhagen and Berlin. Peter the Great encouraged him to follow a diplomatic path and in 1713 Bestuzhev entered the service of the Elector of Hanover, who was later to become King George I of Great Britain. Consequently, Bestuzhev spent several years in England, an experience that was later to influence his foreign policy.

Bestuzhev's early career was very much caught up in palace intrigue and his fortunes were dependent upon which party was in power. He had also narrowly escaped the ire of Peter the Great by corresponding with Peter's son Alexei, when the young man was in Vienna prior to his arrest.

Elizabeth faced two major wars during her reign. First was the War of the Austrian Succession, between 1740 and 1748, ostensibly over Maria Theresa's claim to the Habsburg throne. Second, the Seven Years' War, between 1756 and 1763, which was essentially a conflict between Great Britain and France but eventually drew in most of Europe, the Americas, Africa and Asia.

Russia played a part in both wars. Bestuzhev's inclination was always to favour an alliance with Great Britain and it was no surprise that during the War of the Austrian Succession, with the support of Elizabeth, Russia allied with Great Britain and Austria against France and Prussia with their aggressive expansionist policies.

However, the situation was to change during the Seven Years' War when Russia found herself on the same side as France, her long-term enemy, and on the opposite side of her natural ally, Great Britain.

Elizabeth died in January 1762 following a steady decline in her health. She was surrounded by her heir, the future Peter III, together with his wife Catherine, the future Catherine the Great. Count Alexey Razumovsky, her long-term lover, was also by her side.

Conclusion

Peter the Great has been credited with transforming Russia from being a medieval and backward country into a modern European state on a par with other Western European countries of the time.

But this is perhaps too simplistic a view of his achievements. It might be more correct to regard his reign as the beginning of a process that was going to be long and painful before Russia finally made the transition under Catherine the Great in 1762.

Peter had been ruthless in implementing his reforms. He was committed to secularism and therefore he was particularly hard on the Church and the Old Believers. He ordered the mass movement of people to provide the labour needed to build St. Petersburg and he appointed many foreigners to senior positions at court. Not surprisingly these policies were not popular with everyone. When he died in 1725 the Empire was far from stable, a situation that was to continue for almost forty years.

During this period of instability, six different rulers ascended the throne. One, Ivan VI, was a child of two months. Three, Catherine,

Anna and Elizabeth, were women. Peter II was proclaimed heir at the age of 12 and died at 14 years. Peter III ruled for just six months.

Apart from Elizabeth, the real power behind the throne during these turbulent years was in the hands of a Regent, the Privy Council or senior statesmen. In the case of a minor, for example Peter II or Ivan VI, a Regent was necessary. But the women, whether Regent or Empress, also came under the influence of powerful statesmen who were usually past or present lovers. Since Catherine I was the first woman to ascend the throne after Peter the Great, it might have been considered opportune that a senior statesman should act as her adviser. This was perhaps less important when it came to Elizabeth. As the daughter of Peter the Great she was highly respected by both the Privy Council and also the Palace Guard.

A change in ruler usually resulted in a change in court favourites. Anna, for example, disbanded her Privy Council and had many of them either executed or sent to Siberia. She then surrounded herself with her supporters. With a change in Emperor or Empress there also came changes in both domestic and foreign policy. Peter III, for example, who ruled for just six months, reversed some of Peter the Great's Church reforms as well as forming an alliance with Prussia, the traditional enemy of Russia.

When Catherine II, known as Catherine the Great, came to the throne in 1762, she picked up Peter's programme of reform, modernisation and expansion. In other words, while Peter the Great began the process of Westernisation, Catherine the Great brought it to fruition.

*****

CHAPTER NINE
Catherine the Great

Marriage

The childless Empress Elizabeth proclaimed her nephew Peter as her successor in November 1742, when the boy was just 14 years old. She then had to find a suitable wife for the future Tsar. She chose Princess Sophie Friederike Auguste von Anhalt-Zerbst-Domberg, daughter of the Governor of Stettin (today's Szczecin in Poland), at that time in Prussia. It was hoped by some of Elizabeth's advisers that the marriage would strengthen Russian-Prussian relations and thereby weaken Austria's influence on Russia. Peter, being Prussian born, was naturally pro-Prussian and so the choice of Sophie was acceptable.

Sophie was taken to Russia with her domineering mother in 1744, when she was 14 years old. She had met Peter a few years earlier and had taken an instant dislike to him, largely on account of his early liking for alcohol and bad manners. Despite this, she was determined to do her duty and follow the will of her parents and Empress Elizabeth.

Sophie made a good impression on Empress Elizabeth and in June 1744, she was accepted into the Russian Orthodox Church, taking the name Catherine, despite the protestations of her father, who was a strict Lutheran. From this moment, the young Catherine dedicated herself to being accepted by the Russian Court and the Russian people. She spent many hours learning the Russian language and history, as well as the history and liturgy of the Russian Orthodox Church.

In August 1745, Peter and Catherine were married in St. Petersburg and settled in the nearby palace of Oranienbaum. But it was not to be a happy marriage. Peter's drinking increased, he took a mistress, was vulgar and played childish pranks. He insulted the ladies of the Court by poking his tongue out at them and he made a spectacle of himself in Church, laughing, shouting and insulting the priests.

Consequently, Catherine avoided Peter as much as possible and since they had a mutual dislike for each other, the couple spent little time together. This gave her the opportunity to devote more time to her Russian studies. She also spent many hours reading and was particularly interested in French writers such as Diderot, and she regularly corresponded with Voltaire. In common with Peter the Great, she became dedicated to the philosophy of the Enlightenment.

During these lonely years she found a physical outlet by horse riding. She became a skilled horsewoman and whenever possible would ride alone and astride. This brings to mind another Empress who was trapped in a loveless marriage and found solace on the back of a horse: Empress Elizabeth of Austria, also known as Sisi.

The Birth of Paul

Catherine had never been a great beauty, but as she matured she was described as striking. She had thick brown hair, an attractive face and a good figure that suited luxurious clothes. Above all, she was charming and full of vitality. She enjoyed male company, had many admirers and it was only a matter of time before she started to take lovers.

Her first known lover was Sergei Saltykov, who was appointed Chamberlain, in charge of the royal household, in 1751. He was from a *boyar* family and descended from both the *Rurik* and Romanov lines. In 1754, after two miscarriages, Catherine gave birth to a son. He was named Paul and was to be the future Tsar. Empress Elizabeth had probably accepted by this time that her nephew, Peter, was impotent and that the child born to Catherine was most likely the son of Saltykov. Catherine, in her memoires, claimed that Saltykov was indeed the father despite the fact that as an adult, Paul resembled Peter, both physically and in temperament. Catherine dismissed this by claiming that Paul resembled Saltykov's brother.

Immediately after the birth, the child was removed by Empress Elizabeth and taken into her care. Catherine was to have little contact with her son and Peter, officially the boy's father, was not interested in the baby.

Following the birth, Saltykov disappeared from the scene but it was not long before Catherine had taken another lover, a young Polish count by the name of Stanislas Poniatowski, who was secretary to the British Ambassador Sir Charles Hanbury-Williams.

Poniatowski was a few years younger than Catherine. He was described as being tall and handsome, gentle, highly educated, having a keen wit and was extremely charming. In fact, he was the exact opposite to Catherine's husband Peter. In December 1757, Catherine gave birth to Poniatowski's daughter. She was named Anna Petrovna and once more Empress Elizabeth took the child, who unfortunately survived less than two years, into her care.

Poniatowski returned to Poland and in 1764 Catherine, who by then was Empress and Autocrat of all the Russias, was influential in securing his enthronement as the last King of Poland.

The Coup

The next lover of significance to capture Catherine's eye, was Grigory Grigoryevich Orlov, son of the Governor of Novgorod. Educated at the Cadet Corps in St. Petersburg, Orlov fought in the Seven Years' War. He was one of five brothers, all who held high ranks in the Guards. Their grandfather had fought alongside the *Strelsy* rebels who had been brutally put down by Peter the Great.

Grigory became a close confidante of Catherine, as well as her lover and in April 1762, she gave birth to his son who was named Aleksey Grigorievich Bobrinsky.

On the 5th January 1762, just a few months before the birth of Catherine's third child, Empress Elizabeth died of a stroke. Elizabeth's nephew Peter then ascended the throne as Peter III, Autocrat and Emperor of all the Russias and Catherine became

Empress.

Peter's first act on ascending the throne was to withdraw Russia from the Seven Years' War and make peace with Prussia. He was naturally pro-Russian and a great admirer of Frederick II, King of Prussia, so this was perhaps no surprise. Equally, he might have believed that Russia's best interests would be served in alliance with Prussia and Great Britain rather than Austria and France.

Whatever his motives, the decision proved unpopular, particularly among the military, which overnight found it was fighting an enemy that only days before had been an ally. Peter had also made enemies of members of the Court, especially those who had suffered humiliation and insult at his hands.

Catherine had shown from an early age that she was ambitious for power. She had worked hard to ingratiate herself with the people of Russia. Although coming from a German background she quickly became proficient in Russian and was committed to the Russian Orthodox Church despite being raised as a Lutheran. She had taken a keen interest in foreign affairs and as mentioned earlier, was an enthusiast of Enlightenment philosophy. Her close relationship with Orlov provided a breeding ground for sharing thoughts of conspiracy on how to overthrow her husband Peter.

Shortly after midnight on the 18th June 1762, Grigory Orlov and his brothers escorted Catherine to the headquarters of the Izmailovsky Regiment where she received an oath of allegiance from the troops. The Semeonovsky and Preobrazhenski Regiments followed suit. This was the beginning of a bloodless revolution that overthrew Peter III.

On the 28th June Peter was arrested and forced to abdicate. On the 17th July 1762, at the age of 34 years, he was dead. He was possibly assassinated, or died in a drunken brawl. The real cause has remained a mystery. When his son, Paul, came to the throne, he had his father's body exhumed and reburied in the Peter and Paul Cathedral in St. Petersburg, alongside previous Tsars.

Catherine the Empress

On the 22nd September 1762, Catherine was crowned Empress and Autocrat of All the Russias at the Assumption Cathedral in Moscow. The Swiss-French diamond jeweler Jeremie Pauzie designed her Byzantine style crown that was encrusted with thousands of diamonds from the famous Golconda mines in India. In the tradition of previous Tsars and Emperors, Catherine placed the crown on her own head. Known as the Imperial Crown of Russia, it was used by all later Emperors until 1896 when Nicholas II, the last Romanov Emperor, ascended the throne.

One of Catherine's first acts was to reward her supporters and especially Grigory Orlov and his brothers. Grigory was immediately made a Count and another brother was appointed chief procurator of the Governing Senate. Many other supporters received titles and estates.

Catherine was now Empress, but her position was insecure. She was not a Romanov and not even Russian. Even more seriously, there were two living claimants to the throne, both with a greater legitimacy: the imprisoned Peter III and the imprisoned Ivan VI. When Peter died in July 1762 and Ivan in July 1764, the finger of suspicion pointed towards Catherine and her accomplices.

Catherine's Instructions to the Legislative Commission

Catherine was determined to make her mark as an enlightened monarch. Early in her reign she decided to replace the Muscovite code of laws with a new code more suited to her view of Empire. Known as the Instruction of Catherine the Great, or *Nakaz*, it was modeled on ideas of the French Enlightenment. Grigory Orlov and another close adviser, Nikita Panin, helped her draft the document. The final version, which took her two years to complete, contained 22 Chapters comprising over 600 Articles.

The Empress wrote the original version in French and then translated it herself into Russian. A German translation was sent to Frederick II of Prussia. The first part of the Instruction describes her understanding of the Empire and her role as Empress.

Article 6 states:

'*Russia is an European State*'

Article 9 states that:

'*The Sovereign is absolute; for there is no other authority but that which centers in his single Person that can act with a Vigour proportionate to the Extent of such a vast Dominion.*'

Article 13 asks:

'*What is the true End of Monarchy? Not to deprive People of their natural Liberty; but to correct their Actions, in order to attain the supreme Good.*'

These three Articles alone give a clear indication that Catherine saw herself as holding supreme power over a vast European Empire. She also believed that one of her prime duties was to 'correct' the actions of the people.

Wishing to be seen as an enlightened ruler, she devoted a large part of the legislation to crime and punishment. For example, Article 67 states that '*The application of punishment ought not to proceed from the arbitrary will or mere caprice of the Legislator, but from the nature of the crime...*'

Regarding the use of torture, Article 123 states: '*The Usage of Torture is contrary to all the Dictates of Nature and Reason...*' Catherine specifically condemned the use of the Rack in several Articles, stressing that the accused should receive a fair trial and should not be condemned until proven guilty. (Documents in Russian History, *The Instructions of Catherine II to the Legislative Commission of* 1767)

Fall of Orlov

Although Grigory Orlov and Nikita Panin had co-operated in drafting the *Nakaz*, there were tensions between the two men. For example, they differed over foreign policy. More importantly, Panin, and others, were highly critical of Orlov's relationship with Catherine, believing that he held far too much influence over her.

With the intention of securing his downfall, Panin told the Empress that Orlov was conducting an affair with his 13 years old niece. In an attempt to refute this allegation and reassure Catherine of his affections, Orlov gave her a valuable 189 carats diamond from Golkonda in India. Known as the Orlov diamond, it is now displayed in the diamond collection at the Moscow Kremlin.

But the diamond was no appeasement. Catherine dismissed Orlov with a generous annual pension, money for a substantial household and the title of Prince of the Holy Roman Empire. She then took a new lover, Alexander Vasilchikov, a handsome young ensign in the Chevalier Guard Regiment.

Pugachev's Rebellion

Catherine's reforming policies were not universally popular. The peasantry, the Old Believers and the Cossacks were suspicious of her pro-Western stance that devalued traditional Russian values. Furthermore, many questioned her legitimacy, believing that her deposed husband, Peter III, was the rightful ruler.

While Catherine awarded the nobility with estates, either as a reward for past service, or in the hope of gaining future support, this was often at the expense of the serfs. In the past, they had experienced a degree of security by being bound to the land. Under Catherine's new legislation they were now passed from one landowner to another or simply sold off.

For centuries the Cossacks, who were an East Slavic-speaking people, had enjoyed freedom and independence with their own distinctive identity and language. Living a semi-nomadic lifestyle, the various Cossack communities straddled an area roughly equating to today's Ukraine.

During the reign of Ivan IV in the 16th Century, around 600 Cossacks led by their *ataman* (leader) Yermak Timofeyevich, began the colonisation of Siberia. By 1646 they had reached the Pacific Ocean. Two years later the Cossacks crossed the Bering Straits and settled in Alaska. By the reign of Peter the Great at the beginning of the 18th Century, the Cossacks and their respective colonies were falling victim to the Emperor's aggressive expansionism as he gradually absorbed their towns into the Russian Empire.

By Catherine's reign, there were two major groups: the Don Cossacks of the middle and lower Don region, and the Zaporozhian Sich of the Dnieper region. The Cossack lands conveniently provided a buffer zone between Russia and the Islamic Ottoman Empire and Catholic Poland-Lithuania. Under Catherine, the Russian army recruited Cossacks into its ranks, very often as independent fighting units. The Cossacks fought in the Russian-Turkish wars and later against Napoleon and they became famous for being the most feared and respected among the Russian military, not unlike the Janissaries of the Ottoman Empire.

Unrest among the Cossacks started during the reign of Peter the Great, largely because they were losing their freedom and independence. Under Catherine their freedom was even further curtailed. Everyone suffered an increase in taxation and her new legislation, the 'Instruction to the Legislative Commission', removed the right of peasants to directly petition the Empress or Emperor.

Furthermore, those Cossacks who had been forcefully recruited into the Imperial Army protested at having to shave their beards, wear a uniform and follow a strict military regime. Finally, to add to the general unrest among the population, the middle of the 18th Century witnessed crop failure and plague.

In 1773 a major rebellion broke out under the leadership of Yemelyan Pugachev, an officer who had defected from the Russian army. Pugachev was a Don Cossack who had fought in the Seven Years' War and risen to the Cossack rank of *khorunzhiy*, or Commander. Apart from being an able military leader, he possessed an unusual talent for mimicry. He was particularly convincing at impersonating the imprisoned Emperor Peter III.

Pugachev cleverly combined his military skills with his talent for impersonation. By pretending to be the real Emperor, who had escaped imprisonment, he was able to rally tens of thousands of recruits including runaway serfs, persecuted Old Believers, factory workers, Tatars and non-Orthodox indigenous communities.

During his short reign, Emperor Peter III had set in process the emancipation of the serfs but when Catherine came to the throne, she immediately reversed his plans, an act that added to her unpopularity among the peasants. Pugachev, the 'Pretender' promised to reverse Catherine's laws and grant more freedom and land to all those who followed him.

In September 1773, Pugachev's forces captured Saratov and the city of Kazan. He eventually ruled an area from the Volga to the Urals, establishing a 'government' and military along Imperial lines. His early successes were due to the unpreparedness of Catherine's forces, partly because the rebellion was not taken seriously, but also because Russia was bogged down at the time in a war with the Ottomans.

By the middle of 1774, Catherine's forces were regaining control of the region and in the September the rebellion was crushed. Pugachev was captured, paraded through the streets of Moscow in a cage and on the 21st January 1775, was publicly executed.

Potemkin

Gregory Potemkin, who came from minor nobility, took part in the 1762 coup, the Russo-Turkish wars and the defeat of Pugachev. He became part of Catherine's inner circle of advisers and for a while competed with Catherine's lovers Gregory Orlov and Alexander Vasilchikov for her affections. Orlov had proven to be unfaithful and Vasilchikov had proven to be boring, which left the way clear for Potemkin. He became the love of her life.

Simon Sebag Montefiore, in his book *The Romanovs 1613-1918,* describes their relationship in terms of opposites:

'She was orderly, Germanic, measured and cool; Potemkin was wild, disorganised, Slavic, emotional ...She was ten years older, born

royal; he was the son of minor Smolensk gentry... She was a rationalist, almost an atheist, while he combined Orthodox mysticism with a rare Enlightened tolerance...He had a wit; she liked to laugh; he sang and wrote music; she was tone deaf but loved to listen...She was practical in foreign policy; he was imaginative and visionary.'

Despite their opposite characteristics, they were equals in terms of intellect and sexual appetite and perhaps this, more than anything else, made their relationship so successful. It is possible that they secretly married.

Their passionate relationship comes across in the hundreds of letters that they exchanged. But by 1775, however, things began to cool and Catherine appointed a new secretary, Pyotr Zavadovsky, who became her new lover. Although the relationship between Catherine and Potemkin changed, they remained very close friends even though she subsequently took several more lovers.

With Potemkin's fall from favour, he was able to turn his attention to his diplomatic and military career. He was closely involved with Russia's annexation of Crimea from the Ottomans in 1783 and it is in this context that we first hear of 'Potemkin villages'. According to tradition/myth, Potemkin invited Catherine to visit her newly conquered lands and in order to impress her he created false façades of neat and tidy villages along the route that she travelled. The façades also depicted happy and healthy villagers. This tactic was later used by other regimes, most notably today's North Korea.

Potemkin's name is also famously associated with the battleship *Potemkin* that was named after him. Launched in 1900 as part of Imperial Russia's Black Sea Fleet, the ship became famous for the part played by its crew in the 1905 uprising. In 1925 the event was the subject of the Soviet silent film *Battleship Potemkin*, directed by Sergei Eisenstein.

Russo-Turkish War 1768-1774

By the middle of the 18th Century, parts of the Ottoman Empire, including Egypt, were breaking away from the centralised authority of the Porte, which was the Government seat in Istanbul. The Ottoman Empire was further weakened by Persian attacks under the leadership of the aggressive Nadir Shah. Catherine chose to take advantage of this weakness by seizing parts of Ottoman territory in the Crimea and Caucasus.

Russia's forces were inferior to the Ottomans', both in terms of manpower and naval power and so Catherine sought the help of Britain. Since Britain relied heavily on Russian trade, especially timber for her naval ships and raw materials to fuel the Industrial Revolution, Britain initially agreed. However, when Russia began showing signs of becoming a major power in her own right, a situation that could upset the delicate balance of power in the region, Britain withdraw support.

In 1769 Russian forces succeeded in taking Moldavia and Bucharest in today's Rumania. Catherine also secured a foothold in the Caucasus. While ground forces were active in the Caucasus, Russia's navy, under the command of Count Alexei Orlov, brother of Catherine's lover Grigory Orlov, entered the Mediterranean Sea from the Baltic. Orlov's hope was that the presence of Russian ships in the Mediterranean would draw the Ottoman fleet out of the Black Sea, thereby leaving the Eastern part of the Black Sea, including Crimea and the Caucasus less protected.

Over the next few years, naval conflict between the two powers continued in the Eastern Mediterranean. This was fuelled by Catherine's policy of encouraging and supporting Ottoman vassal states in the Levant to rebel against the Porte. At this time, Egypt and the Levant, including Jerusalem, were under Ottoman rule.

By 1774 the Ottoman fleet was virtually destroyed and the Sultan was forced to agree peace terms that were ratified under the Treaty of Kucuk Kaynarca on the 21st July 1774. The Treaty is thought to mark the beginning of the 'Eastern Question' regarding the partition of a collapsed Ottoman Empire. The conditions under the Treaty included the following:

Article VII: The Sublime Porte promises constant protection of the Christian religion and its churches.

Article VIII: Subjects of the Russian Empire have the right to visit Jerusalem and other places deserving of attention in the Ottoman Empire. They will have no obligation to pay any tax or duty, and will be under the strict protection of the law.

Article XXV: All prisoners of war and slaves in the two Empires shall be granted liberty without ransom money or redemption money. This includes those in the Empire of Russia who voluntarily quit Mahometanism in order to embrace the Christian religion, as well as those in the Ottoman Empire who have left Christianity in order to embrace the Mahometan faith.

The emphasis on the status of Christians living in the Ottoman Empire was a reflection of the growing criticism coming from European countries regarding the treatment of Christians in Ottoman lands. Catherine the Great was to capitalise on the mood of the Western countries with her 'Greek Plan'.

The 'Greek Plan'

Despite coming from a Lutheran Protestant background, Catherine II had always been a great champion of Orthodoxy and she was well aware of the millions of Russian and especially Greek Orthodox minorities living under Ottoman rule. With the encouragement of Grigory Potemkin, her ambition to free these minorities from the Islamic yoke and return Ottoman lands to a restored Byzantine Empire grew. She even harboured dreams that her grandson, conveniently named Constantine, would one day sit on the Imperial throne of a restored Christian Empire in Constantinople.

Aware that this plan could never succeed without the co-operation of other regional powers, she embarked upon secret negotiations with Joseph II, the Holy Roman Emperor. In what became known as the 'Greek Plan', in 1781 Joseph and Catherine signed a treaty formalising an Austro-Russian alliance that was aimed at partitioning the Ottoman Empire.

122

Part of her strategy was to instigate Christian rebellions against Ottoman rule. One such uprising followed the arrival in Greek waters of the Russian fleet under Alexei Orlov in 1770. Rebellions broke out in the Peloponnese and Crete but were put down by the Ottomans. The 1770 rebellions were a forerunner to the 1821 Greek War of Independence.

Partition of Poland 1772-1775

By the middle of the 18th Century, Poland-Lithuania found herself surrounded by three major powers: Russia, Prussia and Austria, otherwise known as the Habsburg Monarchy or Holy Roman Empire. Frederick II of Prussia coveted Polish-Lithuanian ports on the Baltic coast that would be beneficial to Prussian trade. Catherine II of Russia had ambitions of annexing Polish territory as part of her expansionist policies.

By 1772 Poland-Lithuania was virtually a vassal state of Russia, largely due to her success in securing the throne for her ex-lover, Stanislas Poniatowski in 1764. For Catherine, annexation was the next logical step. Furthermore, it was in the interests of Russia, Prussia and Austria, to keep the Polish state weak.

In February 1772, the three Powers met in Vienna and agreed to the partition of the country. In August of the same year troops invaded Poland-Lithuania. In what became known as the First Partition of Poland, Russia seized 30% of Polish territory with 50% of its population. In the Second Partition of 1793, Russia and Prussia annexed further land. The Third Partition of 1795 resulted in the demise of Poland-Lithuania as an independent State when all three Powers seized the remaining lands. Both Prussia and Russia introduced policies of Germanisation and Russification respectively on their newly conquered people, a policy that was aimed at destroying the Polish language and culture.

Stanislas Poniatowski, the last King of Poland, returned to St. Petersburg. Thousands of Poles, including dissidents and most of the intelligentsia, were either arrested or forced into exile in what became known as the Great Migration. There would not be an independent Poland until after World War I.

Conclusion

Catherine died of a stroke on the 6th November 1796. She was 67 years old. During her long rule of 34 years she proved herself to be a woman of many talents. She was highly intelligent, extremely well read, a connoisseur of the arts and an accomplished writer and poet. She also promoted education and commissioned many institutes of higher learning.

Despite her great achievements, Catherine's rule was also controversial. Many criticised her for deposing her husband Peter III who was the legitimate Tsar. Even worse, she and her accomplices were blamed for Peter's death. Therefore some viewed Catherine as not only an illegitimate ruler, but also a murderess.

The mystery surrounding the death of Peter III left the way open for the rise of a pretender to the throne, the Cossack leader Yemelyan Pugachev. He was not the first pretender in Russian history. During the Time of Troubles, no less than three 'Dmitries' pretended to be the real Dmitri who was the youngest son of Ivan the Terrible. (See Chapter Seven) In order to avoid the problem of pretenders, some societies, for example the Mughals of India, publically displayed the head of the one executed in order to prove the real person had been killed.

During the early years of Catherine's marriage, she had time to read the works of the French philosophers. She was particularly influenced by the Enlightenment ideas of Diderot and Voltaire. Once she became Empress she tried to put these enlightened ideas into practice, but she found the concept of meritocracy to be incompatible with absolute autocracy as defined by her Instructions to the Legislative Commission.

Catherine's aim was to 'civilise' Russia along Western lines. But her Western liberal views and certain reforms were not popular with everyone. While the nobility largely benefited, this was at the expense of the peasants and serfs. Pugachev's followers among the Cossacks and Old Believers were equally disaffected.

Her promotion of Enlightenment ideas decreased towards the end of her reign, especially following the French Revolution in 1789. In common with other European monarchies, there was a great fear that Enlightenment ideas had fueled the call for revolution and shock reverberated across Europe following the execution of King Louis XVI in January 1793.

Catherine is remembered in history for her many lovers. The exact number is unclear but it would appear that she was never without her 'favourite'. Some of her lovers, for example Grigory Orlov and Grigory Potemkin, were also close advisers. Others, for example Alexander Vasilchikov, held no advisory role but were short-term sexual partners.

She was extremely generous to her lovers, even after the relationship ended. All received titles and substantial estates. Stanislas Poniatowski received the Polish throne and both Orlov and Potemkin continued to advise her while no longer acting as her lover.

The greatest love of her life was Grigory Potemkin who she may have secretly married. He advised her on foreign policy and took part in the annexation of the Crimea. He was the mastermind behind Catherine's 'Greek Plan' and he was instrumental in founding the cities of Sevastopol, Simferopol and Kherson and also the redesign of Odessa on the Black Sea coast.

Catherine's expansionist ambitions equalled, if not exceeded those of Peter the Great. During her reign, she succeeded in annexing the Crimea and parts of the Caucasus from the Ottomans. Of great significance in this context was the Treaty of Kucuk Kaynarca. Certain clauses of the Treaty relating to Christian minorities living in Ottoman lands would later be used as justification for Russia's interference in Ottoman affairs that indirectly led to the Crimean War in 1853 and the Balkan Wars of the late 18th and early 19th Centuries.

In terms of foreign policy, it is debateable as to how influential Orlov, and particularly Potemkin, were. While the outworking of Catherine's 'Greek Plan' seems to have been the brainchild of Potemkin, he was building on her almost lifelong ambition to see a Christian Emperor on the throne of Constantinople.

There is no doubt that Catherine the Great's reign marked a watershed in Russian history. Under Catherine, Russia rose to take her place alongside the major European powers. At the same time, it is possible to see the seeds of revolution already being sown. Just over a hundred years later a revolution broke out that resulted in Russia losing her place as an equal partner in Europe.

Catherine's reign also witnessed the demise of the once powerful Poland, the largest part of which was absorbed into the Russian Empire, not to surface again until 1918, after World War I.

Interestingly, President Putin is now seeking to regain Russia's place alongside not just the European powers, but world powers. And Poland is redefining herself as an independent European nation that does not want to be controlled by another power, even if that power is a benign European Union. At the same time, in today's Ukraine there is a resurgence of Cossack pride in their history and culture.

*****

CHAPTER TEN

War

Paul I, Emperor and Autocrat of All The Russias: 1796-1801

Within days of his birth, Paul was taken from his mother Catherine and placed under the care of his grandmother, the Empress Elizabeth. He subsequently saw very little of his parents. Whether he was the natural son of Peter III, or of Catherine's lover Sergei Saltykov, Paul believed himself to be the legitimate son of the Emperor and he accused Catherine of being behind his father's death following the coup in 1762.

Apart from blaming Catherine for Peter III's death, which was most likely due to assassination, Paul detested her liberal and immoral lifestyle and especially her string of lovers. He resented the influence that they held over her and he particularly hated Potemkin.

Catherine had never hidden the fact that she favoured her grandson Alexander as her successor, but she failed to make him her official heir before her sudden death from a stroke.

It is perhaps for this reason that one of Paul's first acts as Emperor was to change the law of succession. Under the Rurik dynasty, power had been shared among the various princes, with the Grand Prince taking precedency. When Peter the Great came to the throne in 1672, he introduced a new law of succession whereby the Emperor or Empress named his or her own successor.

Paul overturned Peter's law and introduced what became known as the 'Pauline Laws' whereby the eldest son inherited the throne according to primogeniture. His decision may also have been influenced by his view that a woman, such as his mother, was unsuitable to rule an Empire. The 'Pauline Laws' remained in force until the reign of the last Romanov Emperor, Nicholas II, who was crowned on the 28th May 1896.

Following Catherine's death, Paul had his father's body exhumed in order that he could be buried alongside his wife. He also ordered that Catherine's ex lover, Gregory Orlov, now in his eighties, follow the funeral procession on foot while carrying the imperial crown.

Paul also disapproved of his mother's expansionist policies. He believed that money spent on wars of expansion should, instead, be used to reform the military at home. Consequently, he recalled the troops that Catherine had sent to the Caucasus.

In common with Peter the Great and his own father Peter III, Paul was obsessed with all things military. He particularly enjoyed drills and parades. Potemkin had introduced a comfortable, Russian style uniform for the troops but Paul decided to change this into the stiff, Prussian style that his father had so much admired.

He increased the numbers of parades, that often took place very early in the morning, and he demanded that his senior officers of noble rank take their place alongside the troops. The slightest mistake would result in severe flogging and as punishment he was known to order whole units to march to Siberia, only to recall them after several days' march. He also reversed Catherine's law whereby the aristocracy was exempt from corporal punishment. Consequently, high-ranking members of the nobility were subject to flogging at the Emperor's slightest whim.

Paul had always admired the crusading zeal of the Military Order of St John, also known as the Knights Hospitaller, or Knights of Malta. When Napoleon seized the island of Malta in 1798, the Knights invited Paul to be Grand Master of the Order. Such a role would allow him to combine both his fascination with chivalry and militarism, with being a champion of Roman Catholicism. But Paul's ambitions were to be thwarted. He died before his appointment received the necessary ratification by the Pope.

Within the first year of his reign, Paul passed around 2,000 decrees that affected the lives of all levels of society. He deplored anything French, banning French books, French tutors and even travel to France. He banned the wearing of trousers, frockcoats, round hats, top boots and laced shoes. He imposed curfews, closed social clubs and forbade certain styles of dance.

The Emperor insisted that everyone should remove their hats, and bow in his presence. Even those travelling in carriages were expected to stop their carriage, alight and bow to him in respect. It is popularly believed that on one occasion, he rebuked a nanny pushing a pram because she did not doff the baby's bonnet. The baby was none other than the future poet Alexander Pushkin.

In terms of foreign policy, Paul vacillated between a loathing and a love of France and Bonaparte. While initially forging an alliance with the Austrians and British against Napoleon, by the summer of 1800, he swapped alliances and joined the French against the British. At one point the two leaders were planning to send joint forces, including 50,000 Cossacks, across Central Asia in order to invade British India.

Paul's domestic and foreign policies proved to be highly unpopular and he was increasingly seen as an eccentric despot who was not fit to rule. He had made many enemies among the nobles and high-ranking military elite. His greatest enemies, for example the Zubov brothers, had been loyal supporters of Catherine and her liberal policies. Platon Zubov had been the last of her lovers.

The brothers, together with Peter von de Pahlen, Military Governor of St. Petersburg, started meeting at the home of Olga Zherebtsova where they planned the downfall of the Emperor. Olga was a sister of the Zubov brothers. She was also the mistress of the British Ambassador Charles Whitworth, until Paul ordered him out of Russia when the Russian/British alliance broke down.

The conspirators drew support from the nobility, the military and regiments of the Palace Guard. Paul was aware of the threat to his life and decided to move out of the Winter Palace into the newly built, fortified, St Michael's Castle. On the 23rd March 1801, Pahlen led a group of assassins to the Castle where Paul was hiding with his family. Many of the soldiers were drunk. Some had suffered flogging at the hands of the Emperor. All were out for revenge. They charged into Paul's bedroom where he was strangled and then beaten and trampled to death. The official cause of death was given as apoplexy. He had ruled for less than five years.

Alexander I, Emperor and Autocrat of All the Russias: 1801-1825

When Paul I was murdered in his bedroom, his eldest son Alexander was in the palace. While he must have been aware of the conspiracy to force his father to abdicate, it is doubtful that he anticipated the murder. Nevertheless, the circumstances surrounding the death haunted him for the rest of his life.

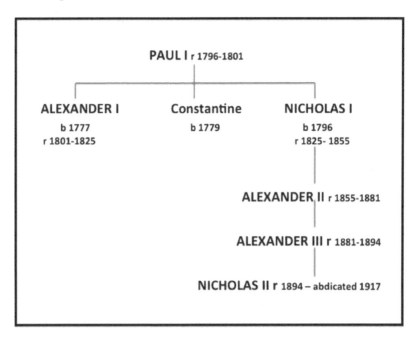

Alexander, along with his younger brother, Constantine, was brought up under the care of his grandmother Catherine the Great. He was a favourite of Catherine and, as previously mentioned, it was generally thought that she preferred him to her son Paul as successor to the throne. Her ambition for the younger brother, Constantine, was that he should inherit a restored Byzantine throne in Constantinople once the Ottomans had been defeated. As part of her 'Greek Plan' she named him Constantine after 'Constantine the Great'. (See Chapter Nine)

Under the supervision of Catherine, Alexander imbibed Enlightenment ideas from his Swiss tutor de La Harpe. His religious instruction was put in the hands of Andrey Afanasyevich Samborsky, an Orthodox priest who had spent many years in England. Consequently, Alexander and Constantine acquired a good command of English. Alexander's military governor, Nikolay Saltykov, instilled in him a strong sense of traditional Russian autocracy and he enjoyed military parades in common with his predecessors.

By the age of 23, when he came to the throne, Alexander was tall, blond and said to be handsome, striking a dashing figure both on the parade ground and on the ballroom floor. But he was a complex character. His remorse over his father's death resulted in an ambivalence to his acceptance of the throne. His Enlightenment ideals proved to be incompatible with traditional Russian autocracy and the type of instruction he received under the priest Samborsky was atypical for the time. To add to these complexities, he ruled at a time of great economic and political instability caused by the Napoleonic wars that lasted from 1803 until 1815.

Within the first few days of his reign, Alexander reversed many of Paul's policies. He freed around 12,000 prisoners, invited exiles to return home, abolished Paul's secret police, restored the rights of the nobles and recalled the troops that had been sent to invade British India.

In the early years of his reign, Alexander had great hopes for reform and improving the lives of the citizens and especially serfs. He set up a small council of close advisers to work on a charter of citizens' rights modeled on the French Declaration of the Rights of Man.

A key adviser, and close friend at the time, was Mikhail Speransky, son of a village priest who had risen to a senior position in the Imperial hierarchy. But Speransky's radical ideas and Alexander's plans for reform proved to be unpopular with the conservative nobility. Speransky in particular was accused of being a French spy at a time when France was the greatest enemy of Russia. Consequently, Alexander was forced to send Speransky into exile in Siberia and his charter of citizens' rights failed to materialise.

He did, however, manage to pass the Free Agriculturalists Law of 1803 that gave serfs the right to purchase their freedom from their masters. But since most serfs could not afford the price demanded, very few benefited.

Military Settlements

With the exile of Speransky and disappointment over his reform plans, Alexander turned his attention to the military and war. He appointed Aleksey Arakcheyev as his military inspector. Arakcheyev had previously served under Paul I and was known to be a strict, to the point of being cruel, disciplinarian. To this day, 'Arakcheevshchina' is a perjorative term used to describe reactionary repression.

Together with the Emperor, Arakcheyev devised a system known as 'Military Settlements' whereby soldiers and their families were housed in special settlements where they were expected to till the land as well as be ready for active service. Local peasants also joined the settlements and sons of both soldiers and peasants started military training at the age of seven years. The aim was that the settlements would provide a much-needed source of military recruitment as well as being self-sufficient.

Arakcheyev was put in overall charge of the project and the first settlements were founded in 1810 in the area of present day Belarus. By 1825 settlements were established in the region of St. Petersburg and Novgorod and accounted for around one quarter of the Russian military force.

The experiment was not successful. Arakcheyev was not an agriculturist. His demands were impossible to fulfill due to his ignorance of crop rotation, soil conditions and the effect of the climate on agricultural production. When settlers fell behind quotas, he imposed severe punishments. Furthermore, due to the heavy demands of toiling the land, the men were then un-fit for military service. Consequently, the experiment resulted in weak farmers and weak soldiers.

Throughout the life of the settlements, riots were commonplace. In every case Arakcheyev responded with brute force. On one occasion, 25 men died after receiving a sentence of 12,000 strokes with a metal cane. In 1857 the Military Settlements were abolished.

Napoleonic Wars

On the 2nd December 1804, Napoleon Bonaparte was crowned Emperor of the French. Throughout the ceremony he wore a golden laurel wreath, in common with the ancient Roman Emperors. He also held a replica of Charlemagne's crown over his head before placing it on his wife Josephine's head. The symbolism of both actions was clear. He saw himself as a successor to the Roman Emperors and also to Charlemagne, the Frankish Emperor of the Carolingian Empire, who had conquered most of Europe during the 9th Century. However, whereas tribes north of the Danube had stopped Charlemagne's advancing troops, Napoleon's ambition was to go much further, and take Moscow.

In the face of the French threat, Alexander joined an alliance with Francis II, the Holy Roman Emperor, and Britain. Britain and France were old enemies and both were competing for trade in the Americas and Asia. Britain therefore supported all alliances against France both in troop numbers and perhaps more importantly, in finance.

Battle of Austerlitz: December 1805

The first major land battle of the Napoleonic wars took place on the 2nd December 1805 at Austerlitz, in the South Moravian Region of today's Czech Republic. At that time, Austerlitz was part of the Austrian, also referred to as the Holy Roman Empire. Alexander I of Russia and Francis II of Austria led the Allied Armies, while Napoleon led the French *Grand Armée*, hence it is often referred to as 'The Battle of the Three Emperors'.

Despite the Allies' superior numbers, they suffered a crushing defeat at the hands of Napoleon, whose battle tactics took them by complete surprise. Leo Tolstoy's epic novel *War and Peace* brilliantly captures the shock and horror of the defeat from the perspective of the Russian soldiers. Against French casualties of approximately 8,000, the Allies suffered over 16,000 dead or wounded.

The battle proved disastrous for the Austrians. Following an earlier defeat at the Bavarian city of Ulm and the capture of Vienna, the Austrians were forced to sign the Peace Treaty of Pressburg. The Treaty, which was signed on the 26th December 1805, heralded the end of the Holy Roman Empire; an Empire that had been in existence for just over a thousand years ever since the coronation of Charlemagne on the 25th December 800. Francis renounced his title of Holy Roman Emperor and thereafter ruled the Austrian Empire as Francis I of Austria.

Treaty of Tilsit: July 1807

In June 1807, Napoleon secured another victory at the Battle of Friedland in today's Kaliningrad on the Baltic coast. With the potential loss of such a vital seaport, Alexander was forced into signing a peace treaty with the French.

On the 7th July 1807, Alexander and Napoleon met on a raft in the middle of the Neman River. It is reported that the Emperors spent several hours in discussion, following which they appeared to be on extremely good terms.

Under the terms of the Treaty, each party promised to come to the aid of the other. This meant that France would assist Russia in her wars against the Ottoman Empire and Russia would assist

France in her conflict with Britain. It was this last point that would later be problematic.

The Treaty also required Russia to hand Wallachia and Moldavia back to the Ottomans and relinquish some of the Ionian Islands that had been taken by Russia, to the French. Prussia signed a separate Treaty at Tilsit with the French two days later.

March on Moscow: June 1812

Although the Treaty of Tilsit introduced a period of relative peace between Russia and France, it was not popular. In the eyes of the Russian people Alexander's capitulation to the French was both shameful and a dishonour to the Russian motherland. Consequently Alexander's credibility suffered.

At the same time, the Russian economy went into decline due to the embargo on British trade that the Treaty had imposed. It was not long therefore before Russian merchants began to break the terms of the Treaty. This was not what Napoleon had expected. He had hoped that Britain's economy would have been destroyed to the point where Britain would agree peace terms with France.

Napoleon therefore decided to force the hand of Russia into breaking off trade relations with the British by threatening to invade. The official reason given by France, however, was the liberation of Poland from the Russian threat.

In what is known at the 'Patriotic War of 1812' in Russia, and the 'Russian Campaign' in France, French troops led by Napoleon crossed the Neman River on the 24th June 1812. His *Grand Armée* was composed of units from territories that he had previously conquered, for example, the Kingdom of Italy and states of the Confederation of the Rhine such as Bavaria and Saxony. His allies included Prussia and Denmark-Norway, making a total of some 685,000 men, although estimates do vary. The Russian army, including Cossacks and local soldiers and militia, numbered around 900,000.

The first battle between the two forces took place at Smolensk on the 16th August. While in theory the French could claim a victory because they captured the city, it was in fact a hollow one. The French had hoped that the Russians would surrender the city and that they would then be able to use it as a base for further incursions into Russia. But the Russians managed to slip away and in the process, burn as much of the town as they were able, so denying the French valuable resources. This was to be a pattern that was repeated over the following months. For example, the burning of Smolensk was an added setback encountered by the *Grand Armée* during its later retreat from Moscow.

For the next three weeks, the French chased the Russians towards Moscow. But their progress was difficult. Heavy rains reduced the roads to deep mud. The munitions and supply carriages fell behind the main army as carriage wheels got stuck in mud and carriages overturned. Consequently, supplies did not reach the troops in the vanguard who were forced to rely on foraging in nearby forests and villages. Unfortunately for the French, the Cossacks had already burned villages along the route so depriving the *Grand Armée* of food and water.

When the rains stopped, the hot sun baked the roads into hard, deep ridges resulting in falls and broken bones, especially among the horses. Disease and desertions followed.

On the 7th September, the French caught up with the Russians at a small town called Borodino, approximately 70 miles from Moscow. The battle that followed was one of the bloodiest of the Napoleonic wars. Both sides suffered heavy losses and at the end of a day's bitter fighting both sides withdrew from exhaustion, resulting in an inconclusive victory.

At this point Napoleon hoped that the Russians would surrender. But following the shame of Tilsit and the retreat from Smolensk, Alexander was unpopular with the Russian people. He believed that if he surrendered to the French, he would probably lose the throne. He therefore decided to retreat further into Russia, but before doing so he ordered that Moscow be put to the torch.

As Moscow went up in flames, Napoleon looked on with a mixture of horror and admiration for a nation that could inflict so much self-sacrifice rather than capitulate to an enemy.

Napoleon waited for a month in Moscow, still hoping that the Russians would sue for peace. With no offer forthcoming from Alexander, he finally decided to withdraw the *Grand Armée* and head back towards Smolensk. It was now October and winter was setting in. His troops suffered from cold, insufficient food and disease. Horses died through lack of fodder. To add to the misery, the retreating soldiers were constantly attacked by bands of Russian peasants and Cossacks.

By November only some 27,000 soldiers were left out of an original force of over 600,000. On the 14th December 1812, the last French soldier left Russian soil. It was the end of the Russian Campaign and was the beginning of the end for Napoleon.

Both sides claimed victory. Due to the heavy losses suffered by the *Grand Armée*, the fall of Moscow to the French has to be described as a Pyrrhic victory for Napoleon. At the same time, Russians commemorate the Battle of Borodino as a great victory over the French in their defence of the historic motherland.

Borodino has been immortalised in art, film, TV, opera, theatre, music and radio. Tchaikovsky's *1812 Overture*, with its use of cannon fire, the chime of bells and brass fanfare, brings to life the deafening din of battle. Tchaikovsky wrote it in 1880 and it was first performed in Moscow in 1882 in front of the unfinished Cathedral of Christ the Saviour.

Alexander I commissioned the original Cathedral in commemoration of Borodino, but his successor Nicholas I disliked its neo-classical design and commissioned a more traditional building modeled on the Byzantine style Hagia Sophia. Stalin subsequently destroyed the cathedral in 1931 in order to build a Palace to the Soviets, which never actually materialised. Construction began on a new cathedral in 1992, which was consecrated in August 2000.

In 1942, Sergei Prokofiev wrote an opera entitled *War and Peace* that was based on Leo Tolstoy's epic novel of the same name.

Tolstoy's *War and Peace* is perhaps the most comprehensive portrayal of the French invasion of Russia. Literary critics and historians have debated as to whether or not the work is a novel or work of history. It is probably a mix of both. Tolstoy began the work in 1862 and while not present himself at Borodino, he was able to interview survivors. He did, however, gain an insight into the working of the Russian army from his involvement in the Crimean War in 1853.

The struggle against Napoleon did not end with the departure of the *Grand Armée* from Russian soil. In 1813 Alexander's forces chased Napoleon's army all the way back to Paris. This was a disaster for Napoleon and contributed to his abdication the following year.

Alexander was then instrumental in forming the 'Holy Alliance', also known as the 'Concert of Europe', whereby Russia, Austria, Britain and Prussia, joined forces in order to combat the spread of revolutionary ideas.

The Crimean War: 1853-1856

The Crimean War was set within the wider context of the 'Eastern Question' regarding the future of a dismantled Ottoman Empire. The greatest fear was that Russia would take advantage of Ottoman weakness by crossing the Black Sea and reaching Istanbul.

The particular conflict in 1853 was sparked off by disagreements between France and Russia over the status of Christians living in Ottoman territories. Under the terms of the 1774 Peace Treaty of *Kucuk Kaynarca,* between the Russian Empire and the Ottoman Empire, Russia was given the right to protect Orthodox Christians living in Ottomans lands. (See Chapter Nine)

In the 19th Century, the Holy Sites in Jerusalem and Bethlehem came under Ottoman rule and under the terms of the Treaty,

Russia claimed the right to protect Orthodox Christians in that region. However, in the hostile climate at the time between France and Russia, Napoleon III insisted that France should assume the right to protect Roman Catholic Christians in the Holy Land. When the Sultan attempted to comply with French demands, Nicholas I, Emperor of Russia claimed this to be contrary to the 1774 Treaty and he threatened to go to war against the Ottomans.

In July 1853, Russian troops moved into the Danubian Principalities (part of today's Rumania) that were under Ottoman suzerainty. Fearing an Ottoman collapse and further Russian expansion, Britain and France rushed to the defence of the Ottomans.

In September 1854, an allied force including the Ottomans, French, British and Sardinians, landed on the Crimean Peninsula with the aim of attacking the Russian naval base at Sevastopol. Over the following eight weeks, three battles took place: at the River Alma, at Balaclava and at Inkerman.

Alma was an Allied success. This was largely due to the men of the 'Thin Red Line', who were soldiers of a combined force of Sutherland Highlanders 93rd Regiment, Ottoman infantry and walking wounded, who bravely held off a Russian attack.

The Battle of Balaclava is remembered for the 'Charge of the Light Brigade', which was a disaster for the British. Out of 670 Light Cavalry, around 270 were either killed or wounded due to a confused order given by Lord Cardigan. The event was immortalised in Alfred, Lord Tennyson's poem of the same name, which was published in the British press just six weeks later.

'Cannon to right of them, Cannon to left of them, Cannon in front of them, Volly'd and thunder'd...

Their's not to reason why. Their's but to do and die, into the valley of Death, rode the six hundred.'

For the first time in history, the reality of war entered the homes of families across Europe within hours of the events taking place. With the help of new railroads and the telegraph, press reports from *The Times* war correspondent William Howard Russell arrived back in London in time to catch the daily press. The telling war photographs by Roger Fenton also circulated widely. Subsequently, the term 'Thin Red Line' entered the English Language as a figure of speech, although the original expression used by *The Times*' correspondence was 'The Thin Red Streak'.

The horrors of war and the deprivations suffered by troops on all sides were now public knowledge, resulting in calls for reform. The poor medical facilities resulted in Florence Nightingale founding a hospital in *Scutari*, on the Asian side of today's Istanbul.

Other legacies of the Crimean War include the balaclava helmet, which is modeled on the woollen helmets worn by British soldiers as protection against the cold during the yearlong siege of Sevastopol. The raglan sleeve is named after Lord Raglan who was the overall commander during the Crimean war. He had lost an arm at the Battle of Waterloo and therefore wore a special coat that was designed to give him greater flexibility.

The Crimean War was a watershed in military history in that it introduced new types of munitions, new forms of communication and eventually new medical facilities. On the Russian side, Nikolay Pirogov, of the Russian Academy of Sciences, developed groundbreaking field surgery techniques.

Conclusion

Following the repressive rule of Paul I, the Russian people welcomed Alexander I's accession to the throne and his reversal of many of Paul's policies came as a welcome relief.

With the French invasion led by Napoleon Bonaparte in 1812, Russia faced its greatest challenge from a foreign power since the Mongol invasion of the 13th Century. But the French invasion was as much an ideological threat as territorial.

Initially many intellectuals had welcomed French Enlightenment ideas. Catherine the Great had introduced French as the language of the Court, and arranged for both Alexander and his brother Constantine to be educated by a liberal Swiss tutor.

However, following the French Revolution in 1789, Russia, along with Austria, Prussia and Britain, was fearful that revolutionary ideas would threaten their own monarchies. At the same time, Alexander, and many liberal minded Russians held ambivalent feelings towards the French and Napoleon. They were attracted by French Enlightenment ideas, but these were incompatible with Russian autocracy.

By 1812, all this had changed. France was now the great enemy and Napoleon was the 'antichrist'. Equally, there were those who secretly admired the audacity and achievements of the upstart from Corsica.

Various alliances were formed to counter French expansionism. But these alliances were against the backdrop of wider issues. For example, the 1807 Treaty of Tilsit resulted in a surprising alliance between Russia and France that was signed in exchange for Russian help for the French against Britain, and French help for the Russians against the Ottomans.

The climax of the war between Russia and France came in 1812 with the Battle of Borodino, and has since been commemorated by the Russians as a victory in defence of the Motherland. Borodino marked the beginning of a new sense of pride and national consciousness in the people. It also led to a policy of Russification across the Empire.

The Crimean War, which followed some 40 years later, was set within the context of Western fears of Russian expansionism at a time when the Ottomans were in decline. It was one of the first wars in history to benefit from railroads, the telegraph and war photography. Consequently, the conditions faced by the troops became public knowledge and led to calls for reform.

The experience of two major wars, within a period of fifty years, resulted in major social problems for the Russian Empire. These problems would contribute to social and political discontent that in turn would lead to revolution.

*****

CHAPTER ELEVEN
Rebellion and Revolution
The Decembrist Revolt 1825

One of the first major rebellions against Imperialist rule was the Pugachev Rebellion of 1773-1775. (See Chapter Nine) The next uprising of significance, known as the Decembrist Revolt, broke out on the 26th December 1825. Whereas the Pugachev Rebellion involved disaffected serfs and Cossacks, the Decembrist rebels were largely soldiers and army officers from the nobility.

When Emperor Alexander I died of typhus on the 1st December 1825, he left no heir. Consequently, regiments of the royal guard immediately swore allegiance to his younger brother Constantine, who was next in line of succession. However, unknown to the guards, Constantine had secretly renounced the throne several years earlier when he married a Polish countess. In the confusion that followed, Nicholas, who was some twenty years younger than Constantine, stepped forward to take the throne.

On the 26th December, around 3,000 troops assembled in Senate Square, St. Petersburg. They refused to swear allegiance to Nicholas, unless he promised uphold Alexander's programme of reform.

The men were led by officers of the Imperial Guard who were members of the Union of Salvation, a group that was dedicated to reform, emancipation of the Serfs and constitutional monarchy. By way of protest against traditional court life, senior officers of the organization frequently wore their swords when attending balls. This was a clear sign of their nonconformist intentions that they would not be taking part in the dance.

Many of the leaders of the Union of Salvation had been members of Alexander's inner circle during the early period of his reign. They had worked closely alongside the Emperor on his draft proposal for constitutional monarchy. However, following the Napoleonic Wars, Alexander became fearful of revolutionary ideas spreading across Russia and he consequently became more conservative and autocratic.

Nicholas, on the other hand, was by nature, an anti-reformist autocrat. Being the third son, he had not been expected to inherit the throne and so had spent his time enjoying court life and following his military interests. Unlike Alexander, who had a complex, but at times an endearing personality, Nicholas appeared hard, cold and inflexible.

When confronted by 3,000 rebellious troops in Senate Square, Nicholas responded by sending in 9,000 loyal troops in the hope that the sight of the armed forces would convince the rebels to conform. After several hours stand-off, Count Mikhail Miloradovich, who had been sent by the Emperor to reason with the rebels, was fatally shot. Nicholas then ordered a cavalry charge to break up the rebels. Chaos broke out as horses slipped on icy cobbles. The Emperor then ordered artillery fire which proved successful. The rebels scattered, many running towards the frozen River Neva. But as the cannon fire smashed the ice, hundreds drowned in the freezing waters.

Nicholas had the ringleaders tried and executed. The remaining rebels were sent to Siberia. The common soldiers, many having received a lashing, were forced to travel into exile, on foot and in chains. The nobility, including Prince Trubetskoi, Prince Obolensky, Prince Volkonsky and the Borisov brothers, was exempt from corporal punishment and travelled more comfortably. Some of the nobility expressed a sense of liberation from the stifling life of Imperial St. Petersburg and Moscow as they travelled eastwards over the Urals and across the vast steppe into Siberia. In a few cases their wives chose to travel with them into exile.

Many Decembrists were sent to work in the mines at Nerchinsk which is near Lake Baikal, in Southern Siberia. Others were sentenced to 'Exile to Settlement', which meant banishment to an isolated village that was inhabited by non-Russian indigenous people. Whatever their social status and wherever they were sent, the Decembrists were forced to labour alongside other political prisoners from Russia and Poland, as well as common criminals.

Where possible, the Decembrists kept in touch with each other, resulting in a growing sense of comaraderie and community spirit, which offered mutual support and a chance to keep their reformist ideas alive. Wives of the nobility who remained in St. Petersburg or Moscow, sent money to their husbands and they continually petitioned the Emperor for leniency in the treatment of their husbands.

While life remained hard for the Decembrists, some of the initial restrictions were gradually lifted and they were able to settle into a more normal, though spartan, lifestyle. They were welcomed by the local people, mixed freely with the peasants and wore peasant style clothing. They became expert agriculturalists and gradually introduced new farming methods and crops. But above all they were passionate about education and founded schools as well as hospitals. The Decembrist wives, under the leadership of Princess Mariia Volkonskaya, were particularly active in founding schools for the local children. She was also successful in her petition to the Emperor, asking that wives may live in privacy with their husbands.

In 1856, thirty years after the Decembrist Revolt, Emperor Alexander II (Nicholas's successor) issued an amnesty to the rebels. Some returned home to their families in the West. Many, however, remained in Siberia where they had made new lives and were able to contribute to the development and cultural life of the region.

It was probably in the field of education and literature that the people of Siberia benefited most from the Decembrists' presence. The works of Pushkin, for example, were widely read. Pushkin wrote several poems that were critical of monarchical rule, which resulted in his exile between 1820 and 1826. If the poet had not already been in exile on the day of the revolt in Senate Square, he may well have found himself exiled along with the Decembrists.

Among the many intellectuals who were supportive of the Decembrists and shared their ideology was Leo Tolstoy. He had friends among the exiles and began writing a novel based on their lives in Siberia. It was later to evolve into his epic work, *War and Peace.*

Emperor Nicholas I died, reportedly of pneumonia, on the 2nd March 1855. He was possibly the most reactionary of all the Romanov Emperors. His rule had been based on three principles: Orthodoxy, Autocracy and Nationality.

His commitment to Orthodoxy led to the marginalisation, and often persecution, of Roman Catholics and Jews. His autocratic rule left little room for the development of a constitutional monarchy, and his policy on nationality, or Russification, resulted in the oppression of his non-Russian subjects. In order to implement his policies, Nicholas employed a network of spies and imposed strict censorship on all forms of publishing.

The succession of Nicholas's son, Alexander II, in 1855, was generally welcomed. The hope was that his reign would bring relief from his father's regressive and repressive rule.

Emancipation of the Serfs 1861

The origins of serfdom in Russia can be traced back to the Kievan Rus' in the 9th Century. (See Chapter One) However, the practice never extended beyond central and southern Russia and consequently the regions beyond the Urals and Poland-Lithuania became safe havens for escaping serfs.

Previous rulers, including Catherine the Great and Paul I, had attempted to improve the lives of the Serfs. But in almost every case, progressive reform failed for fear of upsetting the nobility. The status and wealth of the nobles was largely dependent upon serf labour and consequently they were the most resistant to any kind of reform.

Despite this, by the reign of Alexander I in the early 19th Century, a growing number of educated liberal reformists, including the Decembrists, were calling for an end to serfdom. Furthermore, the Crimean War had revealed the state of poorly equipped and poorly trained troops, many who had been serfs. This was in marked contrast to the armies of their enemies who saw Russia as a backward country that was reliant upon bonded labour.

When Alexander II came to the throne in 1855, he fulfilled the people's expectations by reversing many of his father's repressive policies. His greatest achievement however, was his 'Emancipation Manifesto' dated the 3rd March 1861. At that time, there were some 10 million privately owned serfs, with a further 9 million state-owned and 900,000 owned by the Emperor.

The 1861 Manifesto granted all serfs in Russia full citizen's rights, freedom to marry without their master's consent, the right to own property and the right to run a business. It was hoped that the serfs might become small land holders, which should benefit a market economy.

The sticking point was the question of land. While the nobles could accept the liberation of the serfs, they did not want to lose their land. At the same time, landless serfs posed an obvious threat to social stability and could lead to political unrest. It was decided therefore, that there should be a two-year implementation period during which time a certain proportion of the nobles' land was to be sold to the serfs.

The land was of the poorest quality and it was offered at inflated prices, sometimes 34% above the market price. A long-term government loan was made available to help the serfs with their purchase. However, the strip of land that many serfs received was insufficient to feed their families and the high interest rates on the loans left many indebted for life.

As a result, many serfs found that their lives were no better, and in some cases even worse, despite the new legislation. Consequently, an increasing number chose to leave the rural communities and seek factory work in the growing cities. This was a trend that would later feed into the urban revolutionary movements of the following century.

Polish Uprisings: 1831 and 1863

Following the Napoleonic Wars, European leaders met In Vienna to discuss terms for a lasting peace. In 1815, at the Congress of Vienna, it was agreed that the Duchy of Warsaw, a small Polish kingdom that had been established by Napoleon, should revert to Russia. Referred to thereafter as the 'Congress Kingdom', it was to be held in personal union with the Russian Empire.

Although awarded considerable autonomy, with its own constitution, army, currency and penal code, the Polish Kingdom was in reality a Russian puppet state with the Russian Emperor ruling as King.

Emperor Alexander I had initially accepted the Polish Kingdom's liberal constitution. Nevertheless, he remained the Autocrat of all the Russias and therefore would not countenance any sign of rebellion. His brother and successor, the reactionary Nicholas I, refused to swear allegiance to the constitution when he became King of Poland in 1825. Furthermore, he was determined to extend his policy of Autocracy, Orthodoxy and Nationality, which meant the total assimilation of the Polish people as Orthodox Russians.

The Polish Resistance to Russia's policies of assimilation was met with the abolition of the free press and imposition of censorship. Secret societies, as well as the Freemasons, were declared illegal and Russia's secret police began to carry out arbitrary arrests.

On the 29th November 1830, some young Polish army officers led an uprising against Russian rule. They were joined by people from Lithuania, Belarus and the Right-bank Ukraine, all being members of the former Poland-Lithuania. The rebels held out for eleven months, but were eventually crushed by a more powerful Russian force.

Following the November uprising, Nicholas was even more determined to eradicate all things Polish. He closed down the two universities of Warsaw and Wilna, where generations of Poles had kept alive the memory of a once great Poland-Lithuania; where they honoured the memory of John Sobieski, King of Poland-Lithuania, who had halted the advance of the Ottomans at Vienna in 1683.

With the closure of the Polish universities, young Poles went to the universities of Kiev, Moscow and St. Petersburg. However, rather than becoming assimilated into Russian society, the students held on to their Polish culture and identity even more strongly. Eventually many of these liberal-minded Poles began to influence young Russians with their liberal reformist ideas.

Emperor Nicholas I also dismantled the Polish Army and introduced forced conscription into the Imperial Army. He ordered that all education be in Russian and not Polish. Polish Catholic Churches were handed over to the Orthodox Church and Catholic monasteries were forced to close.

On the 20th January 1863, during the reign of Nicholas's successor, Alexander II, the Poles rose up once again. As before, they were joined by Lithuanians, Belarusians and Ukrainians. The anger over the Crimean War and the serfs' disappointment over the shortcomings of the Emancipation Manifesto, left many Russians disaffected with the Russian monarchy. The Polish rebels had hoped that these Russian dissidents would join them in the rebellion against Russian oppression. When this failed to materialise, the Polish alliance found itself facing a far superior and better-equipped Russian army. Consequently, they were forced to revert to guerrilla warfare.

While Britain and France were supportive of the Polish cause, they refused to intervene. Prussia, under Otto von Bismarck, sided with Russia and permitted the transportation of Russian troops through Prussian territory into the Kingdom of Poland.

The conflict continued until the 18th June, 1864, when the last insurgent was captured. In the aftermath, almost 400 Poles were executed, around 18,000 were sent to Siberia and another 70,000 transported from Poland to various parts of the Russian interior. Nearly 4,000 estates in Poland and Lithuania were handed over to Russians and over 10,000 people lost their lives in the fighting.

Cyprian Norwid's famous poem *'Chopin's Piano'* is set within the context of the 1863 uprising in Warsaw and tells how Chopin's piano was thrown out of a window by Russian troops.

Nicholas I's long-term policy of the complete Russification of Poland had finally been achieved by his son Alexander II. In 1867, the Kingdom of Poland was renamed 'Vistula Land' and was completely absorbed by Imperial Russia.

During Alexander II's reign of almost thirty years, there were several attempts at his assassination by revolutionaries. On Sunday, the 13th March 1881, despite increased security, a group of assassins belonging to the *Narodnaya Volya* (People's Will) party, finally succeeded. A bomb, that was thrown at his closed carriage, fatally wounded the Emperor. The act of terrorism was witnessed by his son, the future Alexander III and his grandson, the future Nicholas II. The event was to have a profound influence on both.

Russo-Japanese War: 1904-1905

By the beginning of the 20th Century, Britain, Germany and Russia were all competing for warm water ports in the Pacific Ocean. Russia had secured Vladivostock in 1860, but the port was ice-bound during the winter months. In 1897, Russia leased Port Arthur, a warm water port on the Liaodon Peninsula, from China. Russia then proceeded to build a railroad to link the Peninsula with the Chinese Eastern Railway.

When the Boxer Rebellion, against Western colonialism, broke out in China in 1899, Russia sent 100,000 troops to join an allied force against the Boxer rebels. After the rebellion had been put down in September 1901, Russia showed no signs of withdrawing her troops. On the contrary, further reinforcements were moved in.

Japan became alarmed that Russia was planning to increase her presence in the region. Russia refused to withdraw her troops and negotiations between the two countries broke down. On the 8th February 1904, the Japanese Navy attacked the Russian Eastern Fleet off the coast of Port Arthur.

Since Britain was opposed to Russian expansionism, she sided with Japan against Russia. Kaiser Wilhelm II of Germany encouraged his cousin, Emperor Nicholas II of Russia, to hold out against the Japanese. Consequently, Nicholas expected German military support and when this did not materialise, the result was a disaster for Russia. Between February 1904 and September 1905, Russia lost almost her entire Pacific and Baltic fleets as well as between 30,000 to 70,000 dead, mostly from drowning.

The political consequences for Russia were equally, if not more, serious than the military defeat. The Russian population initially supported the war against Japan, who was viewed as the aggressor. But as news of successive defeats spread across the country, the people began to blame the Romanovs for Russia's disgraceful defeat at the hands of what was considered an inferior power. The situation simply added fuel to the fire that had already been ignited in St. Petersburg in January 1905.

January 1905 Revolution

Alexander III, who reigned between 1881 and 1894, was by nature a conservative and reversed some of his father reforms. However, since no war was fought during his rule, he has sometimes been referred to as 'The Peacemaker'.

By the time Nicholas II came to the throne in 1894, political unrest was on the rise. In the rural areas, peasants and emancipated serfs had insufficient land for survival and landowners and serfs alike were bound by heavy debt.

Thousands of unskilled emancipated serfs flocked to the industrial cities seeking work in factories, where they became part of a growing permanent working class. If the peasants were successful in finding employment, they joined an army of poorly paid factory workers, labouring for up to 12 hours a day, in unhealthy and unsafe conditions.

Within the military, there was a growing sense of anger at the country's leadership following the shameful defeats of the Crimean War and especially the Russo-Japanese War. Within the universities, students now had access to newspapers and pamphlets which resulted in the spread of new radical and political ideas.

Another significant proportion of the population that was disaffected with Imperial rule, came from the non-Russian minorities. Apart from the Poles, the Jews also suffered from repressive Russification policies. The Jews made up approximately 6% of the population and it was at this time of social unrest that many pogroms took place.

Despite the fact that strikes were illegal, in 1904 mass strikes took place at over 300 factories. Some attempts were made to improve conditions but they were insufficient to appease the workers.

On Sunday, 22nd January 1905, an Orthodox priest named Georgy Gapon, led a large group of petitioners, including many women and children, to the Winter Palace. Carrying icons and shouting 'Long live the Tsar', their intention was to meet Emperor Nicholas II to present him with their petition which called for better working conditions, an end to the war with Japan and universal suffrage.

The marchers were not armed and they were not political agitators calling for political reform. On the contrary, at that point, they were supportive of the Emperor, who they called 'Little Father'. However, when troops opened fire, killing and wounding men, women and children in cold blood, the situation changed.

The event became known as 'Bloody Sunday' and is graphically depicted in David Lean's epic 1965 film *Doctor Zhivago,* starring Omar Sharif.

The horror of 'Bloody Sunday' provoked massive strikes. By the end of January 1905, over 400,000 workers were on strike. By October the number had risen to over two million, bringing the railways to a standstill and crippling economic output. Rioting spread to the universities and mutinies broke out among the naval forces at Sevastopol, Kronstadt and aboard the battleship Potemkin.

Some 20,000 people were injured during the strikes and it is estimated that around 1,500 peasants and workers were executed, with another 45,000 sent into exile.

Hoping to calm the situation, on the 18th February, Nicholas agreed to the creation of a State Duma (legislative Assembly) with an elected membership. But when it became apparent that the new Duma was purely a consultative body with no executive powers, rioting returned. In October 1905, the Emperor was compelled to sign the 'October Manifesto' which granted the people freedom of conscience, freedom of speech and the freedom of assembly.

As a direct result of this legislation, a number of political parties were formed such as the Constitutional Democrats. Other groups, for example the Russian Social Democrat Labour Party, or RSDLP, and the Social Revolutionist Revolutionary Party, became more openly active.

The Constitutional Democrats, also known as the Kadets, were made up of liberal intellectuals and professionals who were committed to full citizens' rights, including Jewish emancipation.

The RSDLP had been formed in 1898 to bring together various revolutionary organisations under one umbrella. The organisation later split into two factions: a minority group (Mensheviks) who believed in democratic socialism, and a majority group (Bolsheviks) who believed in revolutionary socialism. The Bolsheviks were later to be led by Vladimir Ilyich Ulyanov, better known as Lenin.

In October 1906, just a year after 'Bloody Sunday', the Russian Constitution of 1906 was published. But under the terms of the Constitution, despite some concessions, Nicholas II remained the absolute and autocratic ruler of Russia. He kept full powers over foreign policy, the Church and military affairs. Once more, the new legislation fell far short of the expectations of the people.

1917 Revolution

Prior to the 1905 Revolution, numerous revolutionary groups had been operating in exile or in secrecy within Russia. Following 'Bloody Sunday', multiple new groups were established, attracting men and women from across the social spectrum who were calling out for change. The creation of the State Duma and Nicholas's 'October Manifesto' calmed the mood for a while, but with the outbreak of World War 1 in July 1914, the situation grew out of control.

Lenin

Lenin was born in 1870 in the provincial town of Simbirsk. His father was superintendent of schools in the area and his mother was the daughter of a successful German doctor. He received a good education and enjoyed a happy family environment.

His father died when he was 16, but the event that affected him most profoundly was the death of his older brother Alexander a year later, who was executed for revolutionary activities. Lenin went on to study Law but he was under constant surveillance by the secret police on account of his brother's previous activities. In 1887, he was expelled from university and forced to live at home with his mother in Kazan.

It was while at Kazan that Lenin came across the writing of Nikolai Chernyshevsky, social philosopher and leader of the 1860's revolutionary democratic movement. Chernyschevsky's writings convinced Lenin that the future of Russia lay in the lands of an elite group of revolutionaries, rather than an evolutionary democratic process or a mass peasant uprising.

Lenin was in Switzerland when the January 1905 revolution broke out. But on hearing the news, he quickly returned to St. Petersburg and began distributing pamphlets encouraging people to take violent action against the regime. On this occasion, the people were not ready to follow his lead and so he returned to Switzerland.

War

Everything changed with the outbreak of World War I. Following the assassination of Franz Ferdinand, Archduke of the Austria-Hungarian Empire, in Sarajevo in June 1914, Austria threatened to attack Serbia. Consequently Serbia, a Slav country, turned to Russia as the self-confessed protector of all Slavs. Germany then allied with Austria and declared war on Russia. The Great War had begun.

As the reality of war set in, people became increasingly disillusioned. The Duma tried to appease the population by introducing further reform, but rather than receiving support from the Emperor, he dissolved the Duma. When, in 1915, Russia lost Poland to the Germans and the Baltic States to Austria, Nicholas unwisely dismissed his commander-in-chief and assumed personal command of the armed forces.

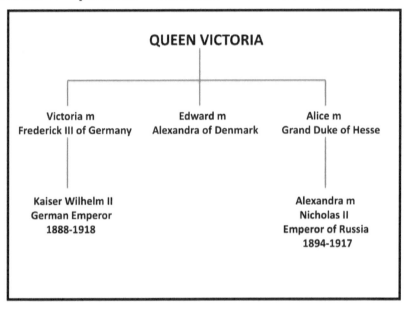

The Emperor spent most of his time at the front and while he was away, his wife Alexandra, who was the grand-daughter of Queen Victoria, ruled on his behalf. Alexandra was extremely unpopular with the people, partly because she was thought of as German, (despite her maternal connection to the British Crown) at a time when Germany was at war with Russia.

But her unconventional relationship with Grigory Rasputin was of more serious concern. Rasputin was a *starets,* a wandering mystic and preacher, who claimed to have healing powers. The young Tsarevich, Alexei, suffered from haemophilia and Rasputin seemed able to bring some relief to the boy. Consequently, Rasputin gained considerable influence over the Empress and some believed that it was he, rather than Alexandra, who was running the Empire behind the scenes.

On the 29th December, 1916, a group of pro-monarchists murdered Rasputin. Apparently, it took several attempts to kill him. When neither poison nor gunfire worked, he was thrown into the icy waters of the River Neva, where he finally died.

By 1917 Russia was crippled with war, with thousands dying of starvation. On the 7th March, workers at the Putilov factory in Petrograd, the new name for St. Petersburg, (deliberately renamed to replace the German-sounding 'burg' with the Russian 'grad') went on strike. Women lining up in bread queues and angry workers from across the city joined the strikers. Within twenty-four hours, the strike had spread to other towns. Troops were sent in to restore calm, but unlike the 1905 uprising, they refused to fire on the people. Instead, the soldiers joined the uprising.

By now the Emperor had lost the support not only of the people, but also of his military. His ministers advised him to abdicate. On the 15th March, 1917, he signed the abdication papers. It was the end of Romanov rule in Russia.

Lenin was still in Switzerland at the time of the February uprising. As events unfolded he was desperate to return to Russia and at this point Germany came to his aid. It was in the interests of Germany to see the Russian government fall and so they provided a train to transport Lenin, his family and close supporters, to Petrograd. It is also possible that Germany offered assistance to Lenin in the hope that once Lenin had secured power, he would seek an armistice between Germany and Russia.

On the 16th April, he arrived back on Russian soil. He received a rapturous welcome from cheering crowds.

The Provisional Government

With the collapse of the Imperial Government, a Provisional Government, made up of many members of the previous Duma, was formed. Its task was to organise elections to a new Duma. Lenin, however, was opposed to the Provisional Government and began rallying support for his revolutionary Bolshevik Party, again with the aid of Germany. At this point, the Bolsheviks were just one of many Soviet (Council) organisations, several of which were opposed to violent action.

By October 1917, Leon Trotsky, another Marxist revolutionary, had also returned from exile. Initially a member of the Menshevik faction, he then joined the Bolsheviks and Lenin immediately put him in a leadership role with responsibility for the militia. Lenin believed that it was now time to take control and oust the Provisional Government.

On the 7th November, the Bolsheviks seized several government departments. They then stormed the Winter Palace and arrested members of the Provisional Government. The Government was toppled and the Soviets seized power in a bloodless revolution.

The following day Lenin called a meeting of the All-Russian Congress of Soviets, where he announced his policies: withdrawal from the War, redistribution of the land, including all Church lands, to the peasants and nationalisation of the banks. Those who advocated a more liberal approach to the revolution left the meeting and Lenin eventually assumed complete control of the Soviets.

As Germany had hoped, on the 16th December 1917, at the instigation of Lenin, a Peace Treaty was signed between the two countries at the town of Brest-Litovsk in today's Belarus. Under the terms of the Treaty, Russia lost Poland, Finland, Estonia, Latvia, Lithuania and the Ukraine to the Germans, constituting more than 25% of the Russian population. The situation was reversed, however, when Germany was defeated at the end of

World War I.

In March 1918, the Bolshevik Party changed its name to the Russian Communist Party and moved the government from Petrograd to Moscow, which was considered to be a safer location. Lenin became Chairman of the Party and Trotsky assumed responsibility for Foreign Affairs as well as the Military. Josef Stalin, then aged about forty, was put in charge of non-Russian nationals.

Civil War: October 1917 to October 1922

The Peace Treaty of Brest-Litovsk was not universally popular in Russia. The majority of monarchists, for example, were against it. Monarchists, mostly members of the Provisional Government and many belonging to the more liberal Soviet groups, were also opposed to Lenin's new Russian Communist Party.

With the collapse of the Imperial Government, all these opposing factions jostled for power. Eventually two major factions emerged. First, Lenin's Bolshevik Russian Communist Party, which became known as the Reds, and second, an alliance of loyalists and liberals that became known as the Whites. The Bolsheviks formed the Red Army. The Whites formed an army with the support of eight foreign nations, including the United Kingdom, the United States, France and Canada. Both sides in the conflict committed atrocities and both sides employed forced conscription to swell their ranks.

By July 2017, the royal family had been moved 'for their safety' to Yekaterinburg, east of the Ural Mountains. However, at the time, the White Army was approaching from the East and the Bolsheviks feared that the loyalists among them would attempt to rescue the Imperial Family and reinstate the monarchy. Consequently, Lenin ordered the execution of the family. On the night of the 16th July, the Emperor, his wife Alexandra and their five children were shot in cold blood. Their bodies were then mutilated, burned and buried in a nearby field. Sixteen days later, on the 27th July, the White Army reached Yekaterinburg.

With the end of World War 1, the Western Powers withdrew their support for the Whites. However, the Civil War dragged on in Russia for another five years until October 1922, by which time, apart from minor skirmishes, the Bolsheviks had eliminated all opposition.

The effects of the Civil War were disastrous for Russia and all the Russian people. An estimated number of those killed in action amounted to around 300,000, with a further 450,000 dead from disease. Under the 'Red Terror', up to one million people, including civilians were executed by Lenin's Cheka (Secret Police). Under the 'White Terror', around 300,000 died, including 10,000 Ukrainian Jews.

Droughts in 1921 led to famine, typhus and death. It is estimated that up to seven million homeless orphans eked out a living on Russia's streets. Up to two million 'White Emigres', largely from the educated and professional classes, fled to the West and the newly independent Baltic countries.

Conclusion

Between the accession of Paul I, in 1796 and the abdication of Nicholas II in 1917, Russia came under the rule of six different Emperors. Throughout this period of just over one hundred years, the Emperors vacillated between radical reform and reactionary repression.

Both Paul, who succeeded Catherine the Great, and Nicolas I, who succeeded Alexander I, reversed many of their predecessors' liberal policies. Alexander II, on the other hand, was committed to reform and it was under his rule that the Emancipation of the Serfs Manifesto of 1861, was passed.

However, even though both Alexander I and Alexander II promoted reform in the early periods of their reign, they hesitated in following through to final implementation. Ever since the French Revolution at the end of the 18th Century, European monarchs had feared that radical ideas would spread to their own country. Consequently, they were cautious in granting too much

160

freedom to the people and they all employed the secret police to monitor citizens' activities.

During the same period, hundreds of thousands of political prisoners were sent to Siberia. The first major group were the Decembrists, the majority of whom were military officers and soldiers who protested against the accession of Nicholas I in 1825. However, it was due to the exiles' presence in remote parts of Siberia that the vast region benefitted from economic and cultural development.

The Russification policies of Nicholas I, and later reinforced by Nicholas II, added to unrest in the vassal state of the Kingdom of Poland. Furthermore, ethnic and religious minorities across Russia suffered from the process of forced assimilation. And it was during this period that pogroms against the Jews became commonplace. The Jews of the Ukraine, for example, suffered persecution by the White Army during the Russian Civil War.

The emancipation of the serfs resulted in major social and political upheavals in the country. While the serfs acquired a degree of freedom, they had very little, or no land. If they chose to remain on farmland, they were forced into financial debt in order to rent or buy a small strip of land from their masters. The nobility, having lost their workforce, also found themselves in debt. Many serfs chose to move to the growing industrial towns to seek work in factories where they toiled in appalling conditions.

By the end of the 19th Century revolutionary ideas, influenced by the writings of political philosophers such as Karl Marx and Nikolai Chernyshevsky, began to spread. Socialist revolutionary groups, both underground in Russia and in exile, were on the increase. Anger over the mishandling of the Russo-Japanese war further added to the people's discontent.

In 1905, Nicholas II attempted to address the situation by forming a Duma, but it was completely ineffective. His October Manifesto, granting a degree of freedom of speech and the right to assemble, opened the way for dissident groups to come out into the open.

The disaster of World War I formed the catalyst for both the abdication of the Tsar and the 1917 socialist revolution. But it was the genius of Lenin that brought the revolution to fruition.

The murder of the royal family marked the end of Imperial Russia, but the beginning of a power struggle that was played out during the Russian Civil War. By 1922, the Bolsheviks had suppressed all opposition opening the way to the creation of the Union of the Soviet Socialist Republics, better known as the USSR.

*****

CHAPTER TWELVE

The Great Socialist Experiment

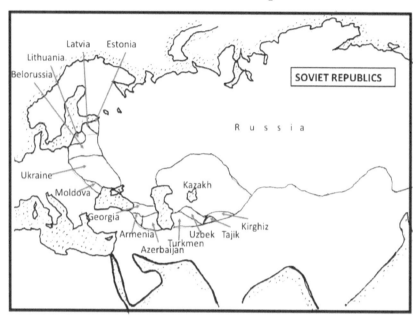

Lenin's Final Years

By the end of the Civil War, Russia's economy was in ruins. In an attempt to redress the situation, Lenin introduced the 'New Economic Policy' (NEP). The most significant aspect of the new policy, which became effective in February 1921, was that it permitted a limited amount of private enterprise and allowed the peasants to sell their produce on the open market. As a further boost to the bankrupt economy, foreign trade was encouraged, but this was strictly under government control, as was basic industry and all transport. For a short while the population was once more able to buy foreign goods in well-stocked shops.

Towards the end of 1921, Lenin's health went into serious decline. In May 1922, he suffered the first of a series of strokes, the last of which led to his death on the 21st January 1924.

During the final weeks of Lenin's life, Joseph Stalin controlled all access, including letters, to the dying man. He then personally made all the arrangements for the funeral.

Lenin's body laid in state at the House of Unions in Moscow for several days, during which time millions of mourners filed past his coffin. The official funeral took place on the 26th January 1924, with Stalin acting as chief pallbearer. The following day, Lenin's body was embalmed and placed in a giant mausoleum where it has remained to this day.

Stalin ordered the erection of numerous monuments across the country in memory of Lenin, the hero of the Russian Revolution. The cult of Lenin was born and Stalin promoted himself as Lenin's legitimate successor on the grounds that he had stood alongside Lenin in bringing about the Revolution.

Significantly, Stalin 'forgot' to inform Trotsky of the date of the funeral. The rift between the two men was common knowledge. Stalin disliked Trotsky's intellectual Jewish background. He also disapproved of Trotsky's policy of recruiting the Tsar's ex-Imperial Officers into the Red Army, despite the fact that this strategy contributed to the victory over the Whites. Furthermore, Stalin saw Trotsky, with his particular form of Bolshevism, as a threat to his own authority

Once in power, Stalin ensured that Trotsky's contribution to the Revolution was quietly forgotten. To this end, he banned John Read's book 'Ten Days that Shook the World' because it portrayed Trotsky as co-leader of the Revolution with virtually little mention of Stalin.

It was no surprise therefore, that on the 21st August 1940, Trotsky was killed in Mexico City by an assassin wielding ice axe. His murder had been ordered by Stalin.

Joseph Stalin

Joseph Stalin was born on the 18th December 1878 in the small town of Gori, Georgia. He had suffered smallpox as a young child, leaving his face badly pockmarked. But his greatest physical impairment was to be his height, at just over five feet tall. His built-up shoes added perhaps another two inches, but his short stature was one element that contributed to his already complex personality.

Stalin grew up in a violent home. His father, who made shoes for the Russian Army, was an alcoholic, and frequently beat his wife and son. He lived in a tough neighbourhood and as a young boy he became involved in street fighting. In February 1892, Stalin witnessed the public hanging of two criminals and this had a profound effect on the boy, instilling in him a hatred for Tsarist rule.

Worried that her son might end up in trouble, Stalin's mother decided to send him to a church school where he sang in the choir and did well in his studies. He had an excellent memory, with a remarkable ability to remember minor details such as dates and names many years after the event took place. It was a skill that would later prove unnerving for those around him.

Stalin's First Five Year Plan, 1928

Lenin had first introduced the collectivization of farms during the Civil War. This involved the seizure of peasants' grain, livestock and farming equipment, as well as the deliberate persecution of the kulaks, who were the better off, and more productive peasant farmers. The Bolsheviks suspected the kulaks of having Tsarist sympathies and also hoarding grain, which was contrary to the spirit of socialism.

The income from the grain seized by the Bolsheviks was used to finance a rapid industrial and military hardware programme. But by 1921, these extreme measures led to famine. In order to alleviate the situation Lenin had introduced his New Economic Policy that reversed some of his more extreme policies. Crucially, he realized that such an ambitious industrialization programme would take generations to achieve.

Stalin, on the other hand, wanted quick results. In 1928, he introduced a Five-Year Plan, and in the case of fertile Ukraine, it

165

was a Two-Year Plan. He imposed forced collectivization and a brutal crack-down on the kulaks, who sometimes committed suicide rather than fall into the hands of Stalin's Party Brigades, which could result in either execution or exile to the labour camps (*gulags*) of Siberia

Once more these drastic measures led to famine. It is estimated that up to seven million people died of starvation, the largest number being in Ukraine. The true horror of the situation was kept secret. Villages of starving people were cordoned off while Western visitors were taken to collective farms worked by supposedly happy and healthy peasants. It was a policy reminiscent of the Potemkin Villages that were constructed during the reign of Catherine the Great. (See Chapter Nine) At the same time, Western dignitaries were escorted round the factories and came away highly impressed with the rapid expansion and high levels of production that they witnessed.

In order to achieve these results, a strict quota system was enforced in the factories whereby underachievers were punished with a reduction in pay or benefits. Even worse, they could be sent to a *gulag*. On the other hand, those who met or exceeded their quota, might be given better living accommodation.

The thousands who went to the gulags were forced into hard manual labour. It is estimated that by 1935, out of some one million inmates, around 100,000 were working on the 140-mile White Sea Canal, that linked Leningrad with the White Sea. The work was completed four months ahead of schedule, but at the cost of 10,000 lives.

Despite the heavy toll taken on the population, or perhaps because of it, Stalin's First Five Year Plan was completed ahead of schedule. He therefore had no hesitation in announcing a Second Five Year Plan which became effective in 1933. Once more the emphasis was on heavy industry and particularly steel-making. Targets, or quotas, were less demanding than during his first Five Year Plan and the provision of child-care made life a little easier for women workers. Under his Second Five Year Plan, Stalin also formalized the liquidation of the Russian Orthodox Church.

The Russian Orthodox Church

At the outbreak of World War I, there were officially 117 million Orthodox Christians living in the Empire, served by around 51,000 priests and 130 bishops. In the early 18th Century, Peter the Great had abolished the Patriarchate and placed the Church under a Sobor, or Synod. However, with the abdication of Nicholas II in March 1917, the Church was free to appoint a new Patriarch. Tikhon, a Bishop who had been serving in the United States, was chosen as the new head of the Russian Orthodox Church. The reinstatement of the Patriarchate did not, however, save the Church from persecution.

During the Civil War, scores of bishops and hundreds of priests, as well as some 12,000 Orthodox laity were executed on suspicion of supporting the Whites. Earlier, under Lenin, hundreds of churches had been closed and the burning of icons and religious books became commonplace. Now teachers were forced to instruct students the precepts of atheism and those who refused, lost their jobs.

During Stalin's rule, the Russian Orthodox Church and all forms of religious practice was virtually liquidated. Out of over 72,000 places of worship before the Revolution, only around 20,000 were still functioning in 1936. Hundreds of priests and bishops had either been executed, sent to the *gulags* or had left the country.

The Great Terror

During Lenin's final months, he became increasingly aware of Stalin's autocratic behaviour, which he believed was contrary to the egalitarian spirit of socialism. He expressed his concerns in his 'Testament', a document that he wrote just before he died. Apart from suggesting structural changes to the Party, Lenin recommended that Stalin be removed from office.

But Lenin's wife, hoping that her husband would recover, delayed publicizing the 'Testament' and Stalin went on to rule until 1953. The 'Cult of Stalin' replaced the cult of the Church. Pictures of Stalin replaced icons and statues of Stalin were erected in cities across the country.

As with most autocrats, Stalin made many enemies. He began to suspect that even those closest to him were plotting his downfall. His paranoia resulted in a large-scale purge of Communist Party members, government officials, military leaders, indeed anyone who showed the slightest counter-revolutionary tendency. On the slightest of evidence, he sanctioned the arbitrary arrest and execution of thousands of innocent people.

Terrified of being arrested themselves, neighbours would report on neighbour. Even family members would inform on each other. Stalin ruled by fear. It was an atmosphere reminiscent of the Spanish Inquisition of the 15th Century.

During 1937 and 1938, Stalin's 'Great Purge', also known as the 'Great Terror', was at its height. The exact number of deaths resulting from his purge is unknown. Statistics vary from around 400,000 up to 1.2 million. According to the Soviet Archives, the NKVD (Secret Police) arrested around 1.5 million people during 1937-1938. Of these, almost 700,000 were executed.

Thousands of skilled workers, peasants, writers, academics and intellectuals lost their lives. But perhaps Stalin's greatest mistake was to purge the army of its most experienced military leaders, just when the country was about to go to war.

World War II

During the 1930s, the rise of the Nazi Party in Germany caused alarm across Western Europe. Consequently, Britain, France and the Soviet Union discussed various forms of alliance in order to combat German aggression. Believing that Stalin had weakened the Soviet Army through his massive purges, Britain was reluctant to ally militarily with the Soviet Union.

Germany, on the other hand, needed Russian grain and raw

168

materials and so Hitler invited Stalin to enter into a non-aggression pact, despite the fact that each country held such opposing ideologies. On the 23rd August 1939, Vyacheslav Molotov, the Soviet Foreign Minister, and Joachim von Ribbentrop, the German Foreign Minister, signed the Molotov-Ribbentrop Pact, also known as the Nazi-Soviet Pact.

Under the terms of the Pact, each party guaranteed there should be no act of aggression towards the other and that neither party should come to the aid of an enemy of the other. At the same time, a secret deal was made whereby should the Nazis be defeated, then the territories of Poland, Latvia, Lithuania, Estonia, Finland and Romania were to be divided between Russian and German 'spheres of influence'.

Just a few days later, on the 1st September 1939, Hitler invaded Poland. Under the terms of the Non-Aggression Pact, Stalin could do nothing. On the 3rd September, Britain and France declared war on Germany and once more Europe was plunged into a World War.

Despite the Molotov-Ribbentrop Pact, Stalin knew that Germany remained a threat to the Soviet Union. However, even though his own intelligence services alerted him to the German danger, and this was reinforced by warnings from Winston Churchill, Stalin refused to do anything that might upset the Germans. Consequently, he hesitated to make preparations for a German invasion.

Operation Barbarossa

On the 22nd June 1941, Germany launched a full-scale invasion of Russia, named 'Operation Barbarossa', after the 12th Century German Holy Roman Emperor Frederick Barbarossa. With three million troops advancing along a 2,900 kilometre front, and backed up by tank and motorized divisions, as well as Luftwaffe planes, it was said to be the largest invasion force in history.

Hitler's motives were multiple: to seize the valuable resources of Southern Russia, to enslave the Slav people, to eradicate the

Jewish Bolsheviks and to spread Nazism through the settlement of German people on Russian lands.

By the 28th June, the Germans had captured Minsk and were heading towards Moscow. The Russian troops were in disarray and Stalin was in despair. However, on the 20th July, Stalin appeared to regain his composure and he took control of the military, in much the same way that Nicholas II had done during World War I. He urged the people to rise up and defend Mother Russia in what became known in Russia as the Great Patriotic War.

Stalin put all his efforts into defending Moscow, being both the capital city and of such symbolic importance. Consequently, when the Germans reached Lake Lagoda, which was dangerously close to Leningrad, he failed to send troops to defend the city. On the 9th September 1941, Leningrad came under a siege that lasted until 27th January 1944, a period of almost 900 days.

Out of a total population of some three million people, only about 400,000 managed to leave Leningrad before the Germans cut off all routes into and out of the city. The remainder of the population endured three bitter winters with very little food or fuel. By the end of the siege, in January 1944, a third of the citizens of Leningrad had died of starvation or disease and 65% of the Russian Army had been taken as prisoners of war by the Germans.

Dmitri Shostakovich's Symphony No 7, 'The Leningrad' was dedicated to the city and came to symbolize Leningrad under siege and Russian defiance and resistance to the Nazi regime. Copies of the score were smuggled out of Russia to Britain and America. Both countries premiered the work symbolizing their support for their embattled ally.

'Not One Step Backwards'

By July 1942, the Germans were approaching Stalingrad in Southern Russia (today's Volgograd). Faced with imminent defeat, Stalin issued his infamous Order No. 227, known as 'Not

One Step Backwards', calling on the troops to defend the Motherland to their last drop of blood. He threatened the death penalty for cowardice and he employed special units, positioned at the rear of his troops, with instructions to shoot any man who hesitated or tried to run away. During the course of the war, around 158,000 Soviet combatants were shot and almost 450,000 imprisoned, for cowardice.

In order to stir up patriotism and a hatred of the Germans, propaganda was widespread. Before the men went into battle, their Commanding Officers frequently read Konstantin Simonov's poem 'Kill Him'. The poem gives a graphic description of the atrocities committed by Germans troops, highlighting the brutality towards Russian women and children. The purpose was to whip up Russian anger and incite an uncontrollable desire for revenge against the Germans

The Battle of Stalingrad marked a turning point for Russia. It lasted from the 23rd August 1942 to 2nd February 1943. Said to be one of the bloodiest battles in the history of World War II, it involved hand to hand street fighting. By the beginning of 1943, the German forces were trapped in the city. Encircled by Soviet forces, and in bitterly cold conditions, they slowly ran out of food and munitions.

On the 2nd February 1943, the Germans surrendered. Around 91,000 men, including 22 generals, were taken prisoner. Many soon died from disease, injuries and starvation. In 1955, following an appeal from Konrad Adenauer, Chancellor of the Federal Republic of Germany, around 5,000 survivors of the battle were permitted to return to Western Germany.

Post World War II

On the 30th April 1945, as the Allied armies approached Berlin from the West, and the Soviet Army from the East, Adolph Hitler committed suicide. Some weeks prior to this, 'The Big Three'; Winston Churchill, Joseph Stalin and Franklin D Roosevelt, met at Yalta in Crimea, to discuss the future of Europe.

However, long before this, Stalin's aim was to bring countries of central Europe into the Soviet orbit. At Yalta, Stalin succeeded in getting agreement to the addition of Poland, Hungary, Czechoslovakia, Rumania, Bulgaria and Albania into the Soviet sphere of influence as Soviet-controlled satellite states.

The Russian people had hoped that life would be easier with the end of the War. But although Stalin could claim victory, he still distrusted his close Party colleagues and he also felt threatened by the major foreign powers. Consequently, he continued with his purges, although not on the same scale as the pre-war period.

When the Americans offered economic aid to European war-torn countries under the Marshall Plan, also known as the 'European Recovery Program', Stalin ordered his Eastern satellite states not to accept the offer. The refusal to be part of the Marshall Plan contributed to the widening gulf between the Soviets and the West. The situation was epitomised by Winston Churchill's statement in a speech he gave in Fulton, Missouri in 1946 that '*an iron curtain has descended across the continent*'. This marked the beginning of the Cold War between Eastern Europe and the West and it was to continue for another forty-five years.

Joseph Stalin died from a stroke on the 5th March 1953. After a brief power-struggle, on the 14th September 1953, Nikita Khrushchev came to power as First Secretary of the Communist Party.

Nikita Khrushchev, Leader 1953-1964

Nikita Khrushchev was born in 1894 in a poverty-stricken village on the Ukrainian/Russian border. His parents were peasants and as a child he worked as a herds-boy. After only four years' schooling, he trained as a metal worker.

Having risen through the Party ranks, Khrushchev acted as Political Commissar during the Russian Civil War and continued in the role during the Great Patriotic War of World War II. He was present at the Battle of Stalingrad and was closely involved in Stalin's purges.

Soon after he came to power, Khrushchev opened the grounds of the Kremlin to the public and ordered the release of thousands of political prisoners, both policies aimed at gaining the support of the people.

By the end of 1955, over one million prisoners had been released from the *gulags* and by 1960 that figure had risen to two million. Many, however, did not return and to this day their fate remains unknown.

As the prisoners returned to their homes, the full horrors of *gulag* life, including forced labour in temperatures of minus thirty, beatings and starvation, came out into the open. Khrushchev ordered an investigation into the situation, the results of which were reported back to the Party.

On the 25th January 1956, Khrushchev delivered a ground-breaking speech to over 1,400 delegates at the 20th Congress of the Communist Party. Known as the 'Secret Speech', and Entitled 'On the Cult of Personality and its Consequences', the content was highly critical of Stalin and particularly his purges of the 1930s. Khrushchev also denounced what he referred to as the 'Cult of Stalin', claiming that this was contrary to the ideals of Socialism as set down by Lenin.

The response among those present, was a mixture of applause and nervous laughter. Other reports claim that some delegates suffered heart attacks while a minority subsequently committed suicide.

The speech was intended for Party members only, but before long it was in the hands of the *New York Times.* It then began to circulate widely around the Communist world. Crucially, both China and Albania, both Communist countries, accused Khrushchev of being a revisionist, which resulted in both countries distancing themselves from the Soviet Union.

De-Stalinisation

The circulation of the 'Secret Speech' resulted in open discussion, particularly among students, about the extent of Stalin's purges and the evils of the *gulag* system. Khrushchev and some of his Party colleagues had been complicit in the purges but now they wanted to distance themselves as far as possible from Stalin's terror. One of Khrushchev's first acts was to improve the conditions in the *gulags* by permitting letters and parcels to be received by the inmates. In January 1960, the *gulags* were finally closed.

The revelations contained in the 'Secret Speech' led to disillusion not only with Stalin, but in many cases with the entire Soviet system. In Georgia, however, the country of Stalin's birth, the people held pro-Stalin demonstrations. On the other hand, anti-Soviet riots broke out in Berlin, Budapest and Prague. The Hungarian riots of October 1956, were brutally crushed by the Soviets, resulting in around 20,000 deaths.

Statues of Stalin were pulled down in towns and cities across the Soviet world. Street and place-names that made any reference to Stalin were renamed. Stalingrad, the city that had suffered the bloodiest battle of World War II, was renamed Volgograd. The final insult for the previous Soviet leader was the removal of his body from Lenin's Mausoleum in the Red Square to an obscure spot near the Kremlin wall.

The 'Thaw'

Despite the ongoing Cold War, Khrushchev was keen to open up the Soviet Union to the wider world and develop a closer relationship with the West. He loosened restrictions on foreign travel for Soviet citizens and he encouraged tourists to visit the Soviet Union.

Unlike Stalin, who had no desire to travel abroad, Khrushchev made a point of visiting world leaders. He travelled to the United States on two occasions and met with Richard Nixon and John F Kennedy. British Foreign Secretary, Harold Macmillan, is claimed to have stated '*How can this fat, vulgar man with his pig eyes and ceaseless flow of talk be the head – the aspirant Tsar for all those millions of people?*" (William Tompson, *Khrushchev: A Political Life*, 1995)

Under Khrushchev there was a flourishing in the arts and literature, the high point being the publication of Alexander Solzhenitsyn's *One Day in the Life of Ivan Denisovich*. The book gives a graphic description of life in a Soviet *gulag* and it sold over a million copies within days of publication. Boris Pasternak's 1957 novel *Doctor Zhivago*, however, was banned on the grounds that it was too anti-Revolutionary. The book was smuggled out of the Soviet Union and in 1958 Pasternak was awarded the Nobel Prize for Literature. In 1965, it was made into an epic film of the same name, directed by David Lean.

The one part of life that did not benefit from the 'Thaw', was the practice of religion and role of the Church. Khrushchev continued the anti-religion polices of his predecessors and during his rule the number of churches and other places of worship, including mosques, were further reduced from around 22,000 to 7,000. The teaching of religion to children, even at home, was banned and the State recorded the identity of anyone requesting a religious baptism, funeral or wedding. Open membership of a religious institution disqualified people from many occupations. Solzhenitsyn, in his book on *gulag* life, describes how Baptists were particularly targeted.

The Space Race and Cuban Missile Crisis

On the 4th October 1957, the Soviet Union surprised the world by launching 'Sputnik 1', the very first artificial Earth satellite. The United States had also been working on its own satellite programme and it was a race between the two powers as to who would be the first to launch. It was never expected that the 'backward' Soviets would outstrip the Americans.

The Soviets also beat the Americans in the second round of the Space Race. It was a Russian, named Yuri Gargarin, who was the first man in space and to orbit the earth. On the 12th April 1961, Gargarin was hailed a hero when he landed back to earth following his successful journey on board the spacecraft Vostok.

Initially the world looked on the Soviet achievements with a mixture of excitement and admiration. Later, however, largely through American propaganda, the Soviet space and missile programme, came to be viewed with suspicion and the Russians seen as a threat to the West.

Tensions between the United States and the Soviet Union were further aggravated in 1961 over the question of nuclear missiles. Fearing the rise of a Marxist state close to its borders, America invaded Cuba on the 16th April 1961 in what is known as the 'Bay of Pigs Invasion'. However, Cuban troops, under the leadership of the revolutionary leader Fidel Castro, succeeded in pushing the Americans back.

Fearing another American invasion, Castro then asked Khrushchev for nuclear missiles. As soviet missiles began to build up in Cuba, America put a blockade around the island. Between the 16th and 28th October 1961, the world watched with baited breath while the United States and the Soviet Union moved closer to a nuclear war.

Following days of tense negotiations, the Soviets agreed to dismantle their weapons on condition that the United States agreed not to invade Cuba. At the same time, the Americans agreed to dismantle missiles that they held in Turkey.

For a while, relations between the United States and the Soviet Union improved, but the affair damaged Khrushchev's political standing. Three years later, in October 1964, he was ousted by a group of conspirators led by Leonid Brezhnev.

Leonid Brezhnev

Leonid Brezhnev was born in 1905 in Kamenskoye, today's Ukraine. In common with many young people at the time, he joined the Communist Party youth organization and he studied metallurgy. He later became an engineer in the iron and steel industry. As with his predecessor, Nikita Khrushchev, he was appointed Political Commissar during World War II.

Brezhnev's style of leadership was in marked contrast to that of Khrushchev in that he was both cautious and consensual. In Khrushchev's latter years he was becoming increasingly unpredictable and autocratic, both factors that contributed to his downfall. Brezhnev was not prepared to make the same mistake.

Soon after coming to power, Brezhnev reversed some of Khrushchev's earlier reforms and returned to a policy of repression. He strengthened the KGB and instead of exile to the *gulags*, which had been closed down, he sent dissidents and political prisoners to mental asylums.

Several years into his rule, Brezhnev did an 'about turn' when it came to foreign policy. In the earlier years, he adopted an interventionist approach. Soviet troops intervened to crush the Prague Spring of 1968 and in 1978, the Soviets invaded Afghanistan, the consequences of which are still with us today.

However, when the Poles rose up under the Solidarity Movement, against Soviet rule, Brezhnev's government chose not to intervene, but to leave the Poles to deal with the situation themselves. It was a decision that would contribute to the later independence of other Soviet satellite states.

Brezhnev ruled as General Secretary of the Communist Party from October 1964 to November 1982. During these eighteen years, although the population enjoyed a rise in living standards, nationally, it was a period of economic stagnation.

With his thick dark hair and bushy eyebrows, plus a passion for wearing medals, Brezhnev developed something of a personality cult. During his final years, his health declined, largely due to being overweight, plus an excess of smoking and alcohol consumption. He died of a heart attack on the 11th November 1982 and was given a state funeral. Despite his repressive measures, Brezhnev rates as one of the most popular of the Soviet leaders.

Gorbachev, *Glasnost* and *Perestroika*

Between the death of Brezhnev and the election of Mikhail Gorbachev, Yuri Andropov and then Konstantin Chernenko, held the office of General Secretary of the Communist Party, for 15 months and 13 months respectively.

Following the death of Chernenko, Gorbachev was voted General

Secretary. He was the youngest ever to be elected to the post and he was the first Soviet leader to be born after the Revolution of 1917. He was born in 1931 into a Russian/Ukrainian peasant family, several of whom died of starvation during the 1932/33 famine.

The young Gorbachev drove a combine harvester on a collective farm and then in his late teens went on to study Law at Moscow University. While at university he joined the Communist Party and then worked his way up through the ranks.

Gorbachev was determined to reverse the economic stagnation of the Brezhnev years. He quickly came to realise, however, that this could not happen without a fundamental restructuring (*Perestroika*) of the Soviet system. A major part of his new policy was the removal of the Communist Party from the Constitution. He also formed the Congress of Peoples' Deputies. Candidacy for the post of Deputy was open to non-Party members and consequently many of those elected by the various republics, were anti-Communist, anti-Government and pro-independence.

In 1986 Gorbachev introduced reforms under his policy of *glasnost* (openness). Restrictions on the freedom of speech and freedom of the Press were lifted. Open debate and even criticism of the Government became commonplace. Not surprisingly, the nationalities of the Satellite States took the greatest advantage of the new situation. Demands for complete freedom from Soviet rule would soon follow.

In common with Khrushchev, Gorbachev enjoyed overseas travel. He formed close relationships with several Western leaders and he and his wife, Raisa, were well received by Ronald Reagan and also Margaret Thatcher, who famously remarked, "*I like Mr. Gorbachev; we can do business together.*"

In 1986, in keeping with improved East/West relations, Reagan and Gorbachev announced a joint proposal aimed at eliminating all nuclear weapons within ten years. Two years later, in 1988, Gorbachev announced the withdrawal of Soviet forces from

Afghanistan.

The Final Years of Soviet Rule

While Gorbachev's political policies were progressive and resulted in greater freedom for the people of the Soviet Union, at the same time the country was suffering economically. The State was heavily in debt and a shortage of basic food supplies led to the reintroduction of food rationing.

The first signs of political unrest began at the end of 1986, with anti-Soviet riots breaking out in Kazakhstan, Armenia and Azerbaijan. Demonstrations also broke out in the same year in Georgia, Moldova and Ukraine.

Calls for full independence in the Baltic Satellite States continued to grow. Many Soviet Satellite States and Republics formed Popular Front movements in order to campaign for independence. On the 16th November 1988, Estonia declared national sovereignty, followed by Lithuania and Latvia in 1989.

As the Soviet Union continued to unravel, Gorbachev came under increasing fire from hardline Communist Party Members. In August of 1991, a group attempted a coup aimed at removing him from power. Gorbachev was put under house arrest for three days. When he returned to the public sphere he had lost all political credibility.

On the 24th August 1991, Gorbachev resigned as General Secretary. The Central Committee and all-party units were dissolved. Communist rule had ended and the Russian flag was raised at the Kremlin.

Conclusion

The Russian Revolution of 1917 led to the collapse of the Russian Empire and the outbreak of civil war. The Red Army, led by Leon Trotsky, was formed of revolutionary Bolsheviks. The White Army, which backed the Provisional Government, was supported by Tsarist sympathisers as well as the Western powers.

With the defeat of the Whites, the Bolsheviks founded the Union of Soviet Socialist Republics (USSR), which was governed according to Marxist-Leninist ideology. Vladimir Lenin, the mastermind behind the Revolution, became Chairman of the Council of People's Commissars of the Soviet Union.

Lenin's successor, Joseph Stalin, had never liked or trusted Trotsky, and when he came to power he ensured that Trotsky's role in the Revolution was quietly erased from history. At the same time, he promoted himself, alongside Lenin, as bringing about the Revolution.

Stalin differed from Lenin in that he was not interested in exporting Marxism beyond the borders of the Soviet Union. Rather, his ambition was to transform the country from backward agrarianism into an industrial power equivalent to those in the West.

In order to achieve this, Stalin introduced his first Five Year Plan, involving the forced, and often brutal, collectivisaton of all farms. The produce from the farms went to the State. He then exported the grain and used the income to finance his industrialization programme. With very little income going back to the farmers, the policy eventually led to famine and starvation.

As Stalin consolidated his power, he became evermore paranoid and fearful of being overthrown or assassinated by his enemies. He instigated a series of purges across Party members, the Military, the intelligentsia and thousands of other innocent people condemned simply by association. Those who escaped execution were sent to *gulags.*

Stalin's victims included the most experienced and capable men of the military, which was a disaster when it came to the outbreak of World War II. With the loss of their greatest military leaders, the Soviet troops were initially no match for the Germans. Faced with the reality of defeat, Stalin speeded up his munitions programme and ordered that any soldier showing signs of cowardice be shot.

A combination of force, propaganda and appeals for patriotism during the 1942 battle of Stalingrad, helped turn the tide in favour of the Soviets. But as at the Battle of Borodino against Napoleon and the defence of Moscow during World War I, the Russian winter, and above all, the resilience of the Russian soldier were the real victors over Hitler's troops.

When Nikita Khrushchev came to power, he ordered the release of thousands of political prisoners. Consequently, the true horrors of the *gulags* came to light and the blame was put on Stalin leading to a process of deStalinisation

Both Khrushchev and Mikail Gorbachev were keen to promote better relations with the West, and especially with the United States. Stalin, on the other hand showed no desire to travel and it was isolationism and a refusal to accept aid under the Marshal Plan, that contributed to the Cold War.

All the Soviet leaders, apart from Mikhail Gorbachev, were born just before the Russian Revolution. Their childhood years were formed during the early years of Bolshevism and they all joined the youth branch of the Communist Party. They also experienced at first hand famine and the Terror.

During the 74 years of Soviet rule, hundreds of thousands of individuals lost their lives or were sent into exile. A large number of these were the professionals, intelligentsia, priests and bishops. This loss of talent and skill must have resulted in an impoverished society. In cases where the visual arts managed to survive, the artists were required to conform to Communist Party ideals, which led to a style known as 'Socialist Realism'.

In every area of the arts, however, State censorship prevailed. Even Sergei Eisenstein's film, 'Ivan the Terrible', did not escape criticism and censorship because Stalin disliked the way that Eisenstein portrayed Ivan, a character who was admired by Stalin.

At the same time, the Soviet period witnessed a growth in industrial output sufficient to equate with the West. And the Soviets can proudly claim to be the first to nation to launch a satellite and successfully send a man into space.

It is now just over one hundred years since the Revolution. The horror of the purges is receding in time and Stalin has been reinstated, largely because he is credited with having defeated the Germans during World War II. The Russian Orthodox Church has been reinstated and the Romanovs have been laid to rest in the Peter and Paul Cathedral in St. Petersburg alongside their predecessors.

Vladimir Putin is now President of Russia. Was the Soviet Experiment just a blip? And is Vladimir Putin the new Tsar in all but name?

*****

EPILOGUE

Following the disintegration of the USSR in 1991, the largest of the Republics, the Russian Soviet Federative Socialist Republic, was renamed as the Russian Federation. At that time, the Russian Federation had the second largest economy in the world after the United States, the largest military force in the world, and the largest stockpile of weapons of mass destruction.

While the Baltic States and most Soviet Satellite States achieved independence after 1991, approximately 20% of the population from ethnic minority and indigenous groups remained within the boundary of the Russian Federation. The majority of these ethnic groups were living in the Caucasus and Eastern part of the country.

On the 10th July 1991, Boris Yeltsin became the first President of post-Soviet Russia. In December 1999, Yeltsin resigned as President and was succeeded by Vladimir Putin.

Vladimir Putin was born in Leningrad in 1952 and studied Law at St. Petersburg University. After graduating in 1975, he joined the KGB's Foreign Intelligence Service and rose to the rank of Lieutenant Colonel. In 1991 Putin left the KGB in order to enter politics. After working for a time in the Mayor's office, he joined the inner circle of Boris Yeltsin where he was 'groomed' as President in waiting.

Chechnya

During Soviet rule, the regions of Chechnya and Ingush in the Caucasus, formed the Chechen-Ingush Autonomous Soviet Socialist Republic. With the disintegration of the USSR, Chechnya, which was largely Muslim, declared itself independent as the Chechen Republic of Ichkeria.

Boris Yeltsin's government refused to acknowledge Chechnya's sovereignty, partly because Russia did not want to lose the region's valuable oil deposits. Also, Chechnya, as well as other countries in the Caucasus such as Georgia, served as a buffer state.

Russia's intransigence towards Chechnya resulted in the formation of an independence movement known as the Chechen National Congress and on the 11th December 1994, armed conflict broke out between the self-proclaimed Chechen Republic and the Russian Federation.

Despite the overwhelming strength of her forces, Russia suffered heavy losses and was forced to concede defeat. On the 30th August 1996, the two parties signed the Khasavyurt Accord, officially ending hostilities.

However, although the Chechens had won this particular battle, they had not won the war. Crucially they had not won their independence and over the following years, the fight for Chechen freedom from Russia accelerated.

In August 1999, Vladimir Putin became Prime Minister of the Russian Federation. By this same time, numerous militant Islamist groups had joined the Chechen separatists and terror attacks in Russia's towns and cities became commonplace.

Putin declared the self-proclaimed Chechen republic to be illegal. In late August 1999, Russia launched air strikes over Chechen territory and in the October, ground forces moved in. By the following May, and at the cost of over 16,000 Chechen, and 7,000 Russian casualties, Putin had reestablished direct rule over the territory.

Putin's perceived hard line won him considerable popularity with the Russian people. The Russian invasion of Georgia in 2008 under his Presidency further added to his popularity as the strong leader that the Russian people both admired and needed. The annexation of Crimea and intervention in Ukraine in 2014, simply increased Putin's popularity at home.

The Economy

The main priority of post-Soviet Russia, was to bring about a smooth transition to a market economy. To some extent, this had already started during Gorbachev's *perestroika* period of the 1980s, when private enterprise was both permitted and encouraged.

Under *perestroika,* entrepreneurs, many of whom held senior Party positions, used their Party contacts and established networks, to set up lucrative businesses. Once the Party system was dismantled in 1991, the ex-Party elites monopolised the privatization of major State concerns, such as TV channels and air transport and gas and oil supplies. Thus, emerged the Russian oligarch.

Those living in the large cities of European Russia, such as Moscow and St. Petersburg, benefitted most from the transition to a market economy. The sector of society that did not benefit, however, included the elderly, the pensioners and those living in rural areas and mono industrial cities. Furthermore, the collapse of the USSR resulted in the end of the soviet welfare system and many people experienced a decline in their living standards.

During Putin's first Presidency, between 2000 and 2008, there was a steady growth in the Russian economy as a result of high oil prices and careful fiscal measures. This resulted in a general increase in purchasing power, once more adding to Putin's popularity with the Russian people. Putin also clamped down on the oligarchs, a move that further added to his popularity.

However, following the annexation of Crimea and intervention in Ukraine in 2014, many countries imposed strict sanctions on Russia. This, together with a fall in oil prices, led to a steady decline in the economy which has been exacerbated by a low level of investment due to widespread corruption. Consequently, Vladimir Putin has suffered a corresponding fall in popularity.

Today

Today (March 2018), relations between the Russian Federation and the West are at a low ebb. But historically this has not always been the case. Russia fought alongside the Western Allies in two World Wars. Ivan IV in the 16th Century, awarded extremely generous trade concessions to the English. In the early 18th Century, Peter the Great established close relations with Western Europe and pursued a policy of Westernisation. He travelled to Holland to learn at first hand Dutch shipbuilding skills and on a visit to England he was inspired by the English form of Government.

During the reign of Nicholas II in the early 20th Century, the monarchs of England, Germany and Russia had close family links through Queen Victoria. In the Soviet period, Nikita Khrushchev had good relations with President Eisenhower and Richard Nixon of the United States. And more recently, Tony Blair and Vladimir Putin were on very good terms. Both leaders, with their youth and vitality, brought a breath of fresh air to politics and it was said that Putin secretly admired Tony Blair.

So where did it all go wrong? A change in attitude was certainly evident towards the end of Catherine the Great's reign in the late 18th Century. At the time, the Ottoman Empire was in decline and Russia and Austria openly discussed how they might capitalize on the situation. Known as 'The Eastern Question', other Western countries, and particularly Britain, became alarmed at signs of Russian expansionism.

Another, perhaps more obvious, change in attitude came following the 1917 Russian Revolution. The monarchical and capitalist countries of the West have always had an aversion to any form of Revolution. The French Revolution in 1789, for example, caused alarm and panic across Europe.

More recently, since the 1979 Iranian Revolution, Iran has been ostracized by the West, even though prior to 1979, the regime of Shah Mohammad Reza Pahlavi was supported both financially and militarily by the United States. Indeed, since that time, the United States appears to have led the way in foreign policy. Put another way, the rest of the Western World, and especially Britain, has followed the lead of the United States.

Returning to Russia, President Putin and the majority of today's

Russian leaders, are products of the Soviet regime. They were born during the Soviet era, educated under the Soviet system and were usually high-ranking Party members.

It is less than thirty years since the fall of the USSR and therefore it is to be expected that elements of the Soviet system are still very much alive, particularly when it comes to the military and secret service. Only when the current generation of leaders have been replaced by those who were born after 1991, will the Soviet era be truly consigned to history. Even then, of course, the Marxist-Leninist ideology that fueled the system will not be completely dead.

In the meantime, Russia will continue to be viewed with suspicion by the West. Russia is blamed for prolonging the human disaster in Syria, despite the fact that her forces contributed to the successful ousting of Daesh. Russia is blamed for interfering in the American Presidential elections through cyber warfare. Britain has accused Russia of using a chemical weapon on British streets, an accusation that has led to a major diplomatic row.

As anti-Russian rhetoric has increased, there has been a corresponding growth in anti-Western feeling from the Russian side. Putin is no longer interested in furthering personal relationships with Western leaders, as he did with Tony Blair. Rather he has become inward looking and conservative. He now extols the glory of Russia's history, encouraging a sense of patriotism and a pride in Russia's past. The Russian Orthodox Church, reinstated in all its glory, has returned to its earlier role, not only as a moral force uniting the people, but also as an Erastian Church that is subordinate to the State.

It is often assumed that nothing happens without the approval of Vladimir Putin. But this is too simplistic a view. Although Putin is projected upon the world stage as an imperial style autocrat, Mikhail Zygar, in his book *All the Kremlin's Men: Inside the Court of Vladimir Putin,* claims that this image was 'constructed by his entourage, Western partners, and journalists' and that 'each of us invented our own Putin. And we may yet create many more.'

Within the next few days, (March 2018) the Russian people will be going to the polls to elect a new President. It is generally assumed that Vladimir Putin will return as President. But many Russians ask, 'if not Putin, then who?'. Besides, Putin's style of leadership is in keeping with a long history of autocracy, whether that be a Grand Duke of Muscovy, a Tsar of all the Russias, or General Secretary of the Communist Party of the Soviet Union.

*****

WHO'S WHO AND WHAT'S WHAT

Alans	Ancient Iranian tribe
Alexander Menshikov	Friend and adviser to Peter I
Alexander Nevsky	Grand Prince of Novgorod
Alexei Petrovich Romanov	Eldest son of Peter the Great
Alexsey Bobrinsky	son of Catherine the Great
Anastasia Romanovna	First wife of Ivan IV
Anna Mons	Dutch mistress of Peter the Great
Anna Leopoldovna	Mother of Ivan VI
Anna Petrovna	daughter of Catherine the Great
Andrey Kurbsky	Friend and general of Ivan IV
Andrew Bogoliubsky	Grand Prince of Vladimir-Suzdal
Appanage	hereditary system under Kievan Rus
Arakcheyev, Alexander	Inspector to Paul I and Alexander I
Askold	9th Century Prince of Kiev
Bestuzhev-Ryumin	Adviser to Empress Elizabeth
Biron, Ernst Johann	Lover of Empress Anna
Boris Morozov	Tutor to Tsar Alexis I
Cumans	Turkic tribe
Danilovich Menshikov	Statesman and Friend of Peter I
Dmitry Golitzyn	Stateman in Peter the Great's court
Dmitry Shemyaka	Cousin of Vasili II
Drevlians	6th Century East Slav tribe
Druzhina	Retinue of Kievan Rus' soldiers
Elena Glinskaya	Second wife of Vasili III

Eudoxia Lopukhina	First wife of Peter the Great
Feodor Nikitich Romanov	Father of Tsar Michael I Romanov
Genghis Khan	Founder of the Mongol Empire
Grivna	Kievan Rus' currency
Godunov, Boris	Russian Tsar, 1598-1605
Godunova, Irina	Sister of Boris Godunov
Guyuk	Batu's cousin and Great Khan
Hesychasm	Form of Spirituality
Huns	Nomadic people of Eastern Europe
Igor	Metropolitan of Kiev and all Rus'
Jeb	Mongol General
Jochi	Son of Genghis Khan
John Palaiologos VIII	Byzantine Emperor 1425-14448
Joseph Volokolamsky	Leader of Possessor movement
Khazars	Semi-nomadic Turkic tribe
Kipchaks	Turkic tribe
Konchaka	Sister of Uzbeg Khan
Kurultai	Mongol grand council
Maria Miloslavskaya	Wife of Tsar Alexis I
Maria Nagaya	Wife of Tsar Ivan IV
Marina Mniszech	Wife of False Dmitri I
Marta Skavronskaya	Mistress and wife of Peter the Great
Magyars	Hungarian tribes
Metropolitan Makarii	Metropolitan during reign of Ivan IV
Mongke	Cousin of Batu Khan
Nikita Panin	Adviser to Catherine the Great

Nikitich Romanov	Uncle of Tsar Michael Roman
Nestor	11th Century monk the chronicler
Nil Sorsky	Leader of Non-Possessors
Ogedei	Son of Genghis Khan
Oleg	10th Century Prince of Novgorod
Olga	10th Century Regent of Novgorod
Olga Zherebtsova	Sister of Zubov brothers
Oprichnina	Territory ruled directly by Ivan IV
Oprichniki	*Ivan* IV's secret police
Orlov, Grigory	Lover of Catherine the Great
Ostermann	Statesman and tutor to Peter II
Pahlen, Peter	Military Governor of St. Petersburg
Pechenegs	Turkic tribe
Perun	Slav god
Poniatowski, Stanislas	Lover of Catherine I, King of Poland
Potemkin, Gregory	Lover of Catherine the Great
Praskovia Saltykovia	Wife of Ivan V
Prokopovich, Feofan	Head of Holy Governing Synod
Pugachev, Yemelyan	Cossack leader
Pyotr Zavadovsky	Lover of Catherine the Great
Razumovsky, Alexei	Cossack lover of Empress Elizabeth
Romanus I Lecapenus	9th Century Byzantine Emperor
Rurik	Founder of the Kievan Rus
Russkaya Pravda	Legal Code o the Kievan Rus
Saltykov, Sergei	Lover of Catherine the Great
Sineus	Brother of Rurik

Skete	Small hermitage for 2/3 monks
Solomonia Saburova	First wife of Vasili III
Sophia Alekseyevna	Daughter of Tsar Alexis I
Speransky, Mikhail	Adviser to Alexander I
Stefan Vonifatiyev	Confessor to Tsar Alexis I
Streltsy	Standing army
Subutai	Mongol General
Sviatoslav	Grand Prince of Kiev 942
Symeon of Polotsk	Tutor to Tsar Alexis I's children
Tamurlaine	Amir of Timurid Empire
Terem	Part of building reserved for women
Tolui	Son of Genghis Khan
Toregene	Ogedei's wife
Truvor	Brother of Rurik
Varangians	Vikings
Vasilchikov, Alexander	Lover of Catherine the Great
Vasili Golitsyn	Adviser to Sophia Alekseyevna
Vasili II	Grand Duke of Muscovy
Vasili III	Grand Duke of Muscovy
Vasili the Cross Eyed	Cousin of Vasili II
Vsevolod Mstislavich	Ruler of Novgorod 1117
Wisniowiechi	Polish magnates
Yam	staging post
Yarlyk	legal document
Yaropolk	10th Century ruler of Kiev
Yaroslav	11th Century Grand Prince of Rus'

Yasa	Mongol Law
Yuri of Zvenigorod	Uncle of Vasili II
Zubov, Platon	Last lover of Catherine the Great
Zemshchina	Territory at time of Ivan IV

*****

WORKS REFERRED TO

A Short History of Russia: Mary Platt Parmelle

All the Kremlin's Man: Inside the Court o Vladimir Putin, Mikhail Zygar

Boris Godunov: a drama in verse, Pushkin, Aleksandr Sergeevich

Catherine the Great: Ian Grey

Documents in Russian History: on-line resource of Primary Documents

History of the Russian Revolution: Leon Trotsky

Novgorad First Chronicle

One Day in the Life of Ivan Denisovich Aleksandr Solzhenitsyn

Peter the Great: Robert K Massie

Putin's Russia: How it Rose, ow it is Maintained, and How it Might End, Editor Leon Aron, American Enterprise Institute

Revolutionary Russia, 1891-1991, Orlando Figes, A Pelican Introduction

Russia at the close of the Sixteenth Century, Fletcher, Giles

Russia: A 1,000-Year Chronicle of the Wild East, Sixsmith, Martin

Russia People & Empire, Geoffrey Hosking Fountain Press, 1997

Russian Primary Chronicle

Russkaya Pravda

St Petersburg a History, Arthur George with Elena George, Sutton Publishing, 2006

Stalin: History in an Hour, Rupert Colley

Ten Days that Shook the World, John Reed, Penguin Classics

The Effects of the Mongol Empire on Russia, Dustin Hosseini, published by the School of Russian and Asian Studies

The Orthodox Church in the History of Russia, St Vladimir's Seminary Press, 1998

The Romanovs: 1613-1918, Simon Sebag Montefiore

The Russian Government in Poland, W A Day, Longmans, London 1867

The Russian Orthodox Church and the Curse of the Mongol Yoke, Article by Alexander Yanov, published by the Institute of Modern Russia

The Russian Revolution, Rupert Colley, History in an Hour

Tsar Fyodor Ivanovitch, a play in five acts. Tolstoy, Aleksey Konstantinovich

Vladimir Lenin: A Lie from Beginning to End, Hourly History

War and Peace: Leo Tolstoy

*****

Made in United States
Troutdale, OR
06/27/2023